D1284583

FROM BEHIND THE PIANO

The Building of Judith Snow's Unique Circle of Friends

JACK PEARPOINT

WHAT'S REALLY WORTH DOING
AND
HOW TO DO IT

A Book for People Who Love Someone Labeled Disabled

(Possibly Yourself)

JUDITH A. SNOW

From Parent Leadership Program 2001

INCLUSION PRESS

First Printing 1990
2nd Printing 1992
3rd Printing 1993
4th Printing 1994
Merged Printing 1998

Canadian Cataloguing in Publication Data

Pearpoint, Jack, 1945–
From behind the piano. And what's really worth doing and how to
do it

"Now in one book."
Includes index.
ISBN 1-895418-38-0

1. Snow, Judith.   2. Physically handicapped — Ontario —
Biography.
I. Snow, Judith.   What's really worth doing and how to do it.   II.
Title

HV3013.S56P42   1998   362.4'3'092   C98-932417-6

Published by
Inclusion Press
24 Thome Crescent
Toronto, Ontario M6H 2S5
Canada

Cover Design & Printing: New Concept, Toronto, Canada 1998

Table of Contents

WHAT'S REALLY WORTH DOING AND HOW TO DO IT 153

INTRODUCTION TO OUR MERGED BOOKS

Since 1991 folks around here have been very proud and pleased with the international response to **"From Behind the Piano - The Building of Judith Snow's Unique Circle of Friends"**.

Curiously, the book is often attributed to me although it was written by Jack Pearpoint -- with much input from me. More and more I am aware that no human being does anything alone. Jack's book is about me, and all of our "company", and has me in it. My book is about Marsha, Jack, and all that I have learned from our companions, and has them in it everywhere. There is no way to say: "This is my work -- that is yours." It is ours, for you.

And so as **"Piano"** is selling out for the fourth time, and **"What's Really Worth Doing**...**"** for its first, we bring them together. As we often say around here: *"Together we are better."*

I am writing this on the day that one of our younger companions died. Maria Galati, aged 19, aspired and passed away to the great sorrow of her extensive family and many, many other people whose lives were touched by hers. Maria was welcomed home from a group home by her parents, Rose and Dominic Galati, her sister Felicia and her niece Maria when she was in grade 1. She started regular school in kindergarten and never looked back. Maria and her parents discovered many of the best practices of Inclusion and taught these ways to hundreds of people. Friends worldwide mourn her untimely passing.

At the same time, parts of these merged texts were virtually prophetic about how disability thinking would lead us again and again into renewed calls for the murder of labeled people -- death disguised as "euthanasia" and "effective human service". Could there be a greater contrast than the Galati family and the Latimer family who murdered their daughter, Tracy, aged 12 in 1994. Our choices are very clear in the late '90's.

Then there is Annie. Nearly 17, she is my boy-crazy Goddaughter, (Mike Green's daughter). She has been to her first prom, works weekly at a day care centre and hangs out with her friends to keep up on the latest music, make-up and movies, She continues to be the delight of her Daddy's heart, and many other hearts as well. Her journey out of "special education" and out of labeling shows that dramatic changes are actually achievable. Annie and Maria's rich lives affirm that it is well worth the revisioning, relationship building, planning, time and effort involved.

There are things I could change in the parts of this book that I wrote. Some say I don't say enough about families. I think it's all about families, but then maybe I could have been more explicit. More could be said about when and what sort of advocacy makes sense. Should I have said more about support circles, especially my own? Are the different ways we use the word "circle" too confusing?

The only changes I decided I want to make are spelling corrections and the alteration of three or four glaringly off-base phrases. Other insights and clarifications deserve a new book -- which will be done in due time

For now Inclusion Press is as proud as punch to present **"From Behind the Piano**..." and "**What's Really Worth Doing**..." **together**. Enjoy. Let the dance continue!

Judith Snow

July, 1998

FROM BEHIND THE PIANO

The Building of Judith Snow's Unique Circle of Friends

JACK PEARPOINT

"There is nothing like a dream
to create the future..."
Victor Hugo

INCLUSION PRESS

Dedication to

Father Patrick Mackan, CR

Friend, Mentor, Colleague

Yesterday, hours after I took this book to press, Father Patrick Mackan, my friend, mentor and colleague arrived at our house. Patrick, with Judith Snow, Marsha and myself was one of the founders of the Centre for Integrated Education and Community. At that time, there was no dedication. Now there is.

We went to dinner together. Pat was excited about the decade ahead. His new mission as "spiritual mentor" - to create a world where all kids belong together.

After dinner, Pat installed himself on our bed, to watch his video tape "Kids Belong Together" with an Australian friend who was eating up his words excitedly.

He had been having leg troubles, so he asked me to help him walk to the window to get a breath of fresh air. Pat took in a deep breath, and collapsed in my arms. He died there - in my arms.

He had a wonderful day - and a great life. He is a great spiritual leader and is with us forever more. He wanted to be with his community - his circle - and he died in our arms. The wind chimes on the back porch had been quiet all day, but they suddenly began to ring - and continued throughout the night.

Patrick is at peace. He also is working on his chosen vocation - in a way I had not understood. He talked of being a spiritual mentor, and he meant it. He is very with us now - and through the work of the Centre - forever.

It was a privilege to have him die in my arms and breathe his spirit into Marsha and I - and all of us who are committed to building a world where "kids belong together".

Jack Pearpoint Nov. 24, 1990.

Prologue
For the 2nd edition (1992)

We are amazed and delighted. 4000 copies of this book have been sold! We decided to reprint because of letters and calls telling how this little book made a difference in someone's life. That is reason enough.

Judith, Marsha and I talked about whether to add new information, or simply to insert a brief prologue. We agreed on a prologue and began to discuss content. We were getting bogged down when Judith suggested, "The Centre's first Annual Meeting last Saturday. That would be a comprehensive update."

Thus, our prologue begins on Jan. 11, 1992, with the first Annual Meeting of the Centre for Integrated Education and Community. We are now a full fledged charity. We are the proud parents of Inclusion Press. The new Board - our circle of friends - says it all. Gary Bunch, recently retired Chairman of the Board of Governors of Frontier College is the Chair. Marsha is Secretary-Treasurer. Jack functions as Executive Director. Rose Galati, Stan and Marthe Woronko have been our teachers and friends as we advocated for their children. They are now Directors on our Board. Judith cannot be on the Board since she is an employee. We appointed her Visiting Scholar. Perhaps most important, Pat Mackan, our other founder was very present. Gordon Mackan, Pat's brother, began the meeting by reflecting on how delighted Pat would have been that Gordon is on the Board too.

The Centre is thriving. We are continuing to invent our own future. Together we are dedicated to establishing a world where everyone is welcome and a contributing citizen. This story began with rescuing Judith from the chronic care hospital, It continues today with our Circle of Friends working, living and laughing - together.

Jack Pearpoint, Judith Snow & Marsha Forest

INTRODUCTION

It is a little embarrassing for me to have a book about me - distributed to the public. My WASP roots cause me to feel uncomfortable with that much attention. After all, nothing I have ever done or been (so far) has seemed so unusual to me. I just get bored easily, and life in an institution with no friends and nothing to do is not a thing I can tolerate for very long.

But even I can admit that my story is worth telling. For 10 years in one workshop after another, Marsha, Jack, the two Peter's and I have been telling the unfolding tale, then listening and watching as it filled audiences with new hope. When many people have heard about the Joshua Committee and my struggle to be truly myself, they have come away with visions of new opportunities for their own lives. Some have conquered critical barriers, others have built new more powerful friendships, and even others have seen different possibilities and gifts in themselves and those they labelled as problems and rejects. If my story can energize people so powerfully, then let it be told far and wide.

But there is another reason why I think my story should be told. Let me add a little of the story behind the story. This book is also about a piece of the life of Jack Pearpoint, fifteen years the President of Frontier College and administrative genius behind my ever evolving attendant care service, a founding member of the Joshua Committee and a friend for 12 years.

Did I say friend for 12 years? As Marsha, Jack and I sat at a shady table on a perfect July day sharing Chinese tea and editing draft copy, we talked about us. How difficult it has been for either Jack or me to admit to and enjoy our friendship! We talked about how our shared Protestant background makes it hard for us to notice or express our feelings, especially the good ones. We talked about getting beyond the roles and stereotypes; was I just a charity case to him and he the always superior helper? As a Western male, was he to settle for being competent, brilliant and alone, or did he also long for trust and love? Could I let my guard down and trust that he wouldn't abandon me for a new project?

Life has brought the three of us a lot of trouble in the last two years. We have weathered it together. As part of coping, Jack decided to write down the stories of his friends. This is one of those stories. It hasn't been easy for either of us to notice and enjoy our friendship. But in writing, reading, and re-writing this story together, we have given each other the best opportunity ever to understand and enjoy each other. Yes, we really have been great friends for 12 years.

This just may be the most powerful friendship story you have ever read.

Judith A. Snow
Dec. 1990
Toronto

In the Beginning
We Met Judith

I Get the First Word...

This is a story about my recollection of the evolution of
my friendship with a remarkable woman, Judith Snow. It is
also the story of the genesis of the "Joshua Committee". The
Joshua Committee was a "support circle" that evolved around
Judith. None of us knew it at the time, but when Judith
dubbed us the Joshua Committee because we "knocked down
the walls", we were experimenting with "circles of friends"
as a support structure. It worked. The interesting thing is that
we started out circling Judith to support her. Now, we have
discovered that we support each other - according to need.
We struggle through the difficult times, and we celebrate life
together - because we are friends.

This is Judith's story - the story of the Joshua Committee
- as seen and understood by me, as we shared life experiences

and friendship. It is not a biography. There is no attempt to be unbiased. I haven't even touched the fascinating history that allowed Judith to survive until we met. The tale of invincible commitment by her parents is not touched. That is another story that needs to be told.

I gave this manuscript to several friends for comments. Several amendments have emerged. Firstly, this story has an "Afterward" written by John O'Brien, a problem solver from Atlanta who travels the world creating strategies to support people at risk. Both Judith and I appreciate that John made the time to reflect on this story. Now we can all benefit from the clarity of his thought.

The second comment was that I needed to introduce the cast of characters in this real life drama. I had struggled with this dilemma earlier, then abandoned it. I didn't want to "label" Judith except as a friend and colleague. I wanted the story itself to be my description of Judith. However, in real life, chances are you don't know Judith, so I am making a compromise. I have added a special two part appendix, following John's Afterward, so that you can check Judith out yourself. You can meet her from at least two diametrically opposed perspectives. Then you decide how to label Judith however you choose. Appendix 1-A is a copy of a speech (the Bradwin Address) delivered by Judith in Sept. 1988. It is an introduction to Judith. Appendix 1-B is another perspective - a summary of Judith condensed from medical charts. You decide what labels fit.

Two other actors play central roles throughout. There is "Marsha", Marsha Forest, who is omnipresent. She was not conjured up as a dramatic vehicle for the story. Marsha is very real. Without her none of this would have happened. And as much as Marsha is the leading supporting actress with

Judith, she is also my leading support. She is my best friend, my most trusted colleague and my wife. Our little threesome is really very tight. We work together, we play together, and we rejoice and struggle together. Related to all this, Marsha is one of the leading advocates and speakers on integration and inclusion. She writes, speaks and advocates internationally. Together with Judith, Patrick Mackan and I, we are the core of the Centre for Integrated Education and Community.

In addition to being the writer, I am the third actor in the book. I am beginning a new stage of my working career, and this book is the first result. I was involved in the management of voluntary agencies in the human service sector nationally and internationally for the past 23 years. For the past 15, I was the President of Frontier College, a national voluntary organization focused on literacy and the needs of marginalized people in Canada. After 15 years, it is time for a change. Part one of that shift is to write some of the stories that I have been privileged to live and to learn. Judith's story is the first.

We All Need Friends - I Have Judith...

I have talked about Judith Snow a great deal. Occasionally, I have written about her. But until now, I didn't try to understand how Judith helped to shape my life and my work. At first it was indirectly, then directly. When Judith gave the Bradwin Address (Appendix 1-A) at the Frontier College Annual Meeting in October 1988, we reached a new plain. It was no longer just the College and I impacting on Judith. She returned the favour - full circle. But, we were a long time getting there. That is the story...

Since my own rhetoric is that one should listen to people, I am reluctantly introducing Judith before I tell her story. Here is how Judith introduced herself recently.

"Once my father told me that in ancient China the very rich or powerful families would bind the feet of young girls. As these girls grew up they became increasingly unable to walk more than a few hobbled steps. But if a woman were truly rich and powerful, she would give up walking altogether and she would also grow her finger nails until her hands were heavy and functionless. She would be carried about all day by slaves who bore her chair and cushions to support her hands. They would feed her and look after her every need.

Now what is interesting to me about this fact, and probably why my father told me about it, is that my body works as if I were one of those ancient Chinese ladies. I get around in a fancy motorized wheelchair and a van adapted with a lift for a wheelchair. I type on a computer with a breath control that reads the puffs and sips on a straw as Morse Code and translates the code into letters and computer controls. Otherwise my every physical need including driving the van must be met by a team of attendants. These attendants cover a 24 hour shift and wages are funded with government dollars.

One critical difference between my life and that of an ancient Chinese lady is that she was considered to be of value in her society just because she was there. Not only was her potential contribution of no concern to the world of her day, but she was actively discouraged from being a direct contributor. In my world, people are valued according to their conspicuous function and activity. Few things are viewed more negatively than disability in my society, where people with apparent disabilities are usually subjected to endless efforts to cure them, or to educate them out of their differences. ... Others are denied ordinary health care or important services, leading to death from treatable infections, starvation, etc."

That is Judith talking. You can see an alternative description (the list of her medical disabilities) in the appendix 1-B. However, I hope you have already grasped the enormous intellect of my friend Judith. You already know why I was compelled to write. So on with the story.

Nobody Said It Would Be a Tea Party

It was late 1978 when I first heard of Judith Snow through Marsha Forest, my wife, friend and colleague. "I met the most amazing woman. She's brilliant - and she drives her electric wheelchair with her thumb." Marsha invited Judith to help teach some of her education classes at York University. From Marsha's perspective, it seemed like a good idea for teachers majoring in "special education" to actually meet some people who were "special". Marsha had the heretical notion that it would be good for student teachers in special education to actually meet some "graduates" of special education, and spend time with the kinds of children and families that they were choosing to be involved with for the balance of their careers. To me, this was good common sense. To the University, it was virtually unthinkable. Imagine, inviting handicapped people to talk about handicaps. What could they possibly know? "They" wouldn't be understood. "They" would frighten the students. "They" weren't qualified. The list of excuses was endless. It translated into fear of the unknown and "they are not welcome".

Judith was one such person. Judith's intellect is a formidable force, but her very "presence" also carries a tremendous impact. It took me years to begin to understand that.

The way this story really began was when Marsha and I went to visit Judith at home - in the geriatric ward of West Park Hospital. It was surreal. Nothing made any sense. I hadn't known Judith very long, but during university, I had worked at Camp Easter Seal in Watrous, Saskatchewan. I understood the difference between a person who was sick and a person who had a disability that required someone else's hands or feet to do certain tasks for them. Judith was 28, in good health, working full time, and needed attendant care for virtually all bodily functions. This wasn't a "medical" problem. You don't need a doctor and a nurse to get you out of bed, help you to eat, or to give you a bedpan.

We visited Judith a few times there, not many. I have never liked visiting hospitals. Still, the memories stick. The first was Judith's reaction when we asked her, "Why are you living here? This is crazy." She was in total agreement. But, since she had exhausted all the attendant care options available in Canada, this was the end of the line. It was ridiculous, but either no one else saw it that way, or no one said so. Judith was clearly "a terminal spinal something or other". Her prognosis was early death (by 30 they told her). So there was nothing to do but sit it out and wait for her death on her 30th birthday on Oct. 29, 1979.

Judith shared a double with an elderly woman who screamed and moaned endlessly. Her roommate was 102 and waiting to die - if they would only let her. Her pain was visible and audible. But Judith was a working woman. She had no control over the muscles in her arms or legs, so she needed to be fitted into her back brace and wheelchair, fed, put on the bedpan, etc. She was a creative woman - teaching at York and directing the Centre for Special Services for Handicapped Students which she had founded. She did not deserve or need to be living (dying) on a geriatric ward. No one does! Judith was both stunned and relieved at our reactions. "Maybe I'm not going crazy after all. Everyone around here thinks I should be grateful for being made miserable and prepared for my death."

The situation was crazy making. We saw Judith as a profound visionary thinker. Many other people were only able to see the enormity of her physical handicaps. But over these 12 years, we have been involved in a never ending saga of "pioneering" triumphs - the first Order in Council in Canada for attendant care, the first private attendant care system, the first Joshua Committee. The first - over and over and over. Simultaneously, Judith is also one of the most physically handicapped people living outside an institution in Canada.

I am getting ahead of myself. I want to recall our beginnings. This is hard to write, because the people and issues hardest to write about are those closest to my heart. I have no perspective - no place to begin - no place to end. It is hard to write about the "omnipresent". So I pluck up my courage to relate the story of one of my greatest teachers and friends - Judith Snow.

I Met Judith in 1979...

I don't have a vivid memory of meeting Judith (then Judy) Snow for the first time. I think it was at a planning meeting at York University. She was then the Director of the Centre for Handicapped Students, and I was the President of Frontier College. A group of us had gathered to discuss a summer project for the Options Program. That was how Marsha met Judith. Options wanted to run courses that included issues regarding disabilities, and they needed a bonafide professor to certify and/or teach the course. Judith and Norman Kunc approached Marsha, then a "real" professor at York.

The courses proceeded, and Marsha invited Judith and others to lecture. From that simple beginning, a new world began for all of us. As Marsha and Judith's mutual trust grew ever so slowly, other options emerged. One was a summer grant proposal, and I was invited to the meeting to explore it.

I was checking my facts with Judith the other day, and trying to recall that first meeting. She was surprised how vague I was. She expected that the image of a severely handicapped woman in a wheelchair would have been etched in my memory forever. But it wasn't. I remembered the meeting. There were several people there - all bright and full of ideas. That is what I remember more than the fact that some people were in wheelchairs, others spoke with difficulty because of cerebral palsy, etc. I was shocked that Judith was shocked. She liked it that my memory was of her ideas and personality, and not her physical disability.

The project went ahead. Students were employed to research the potential job market for students with disabilities. They used a highly experimental measure. They walked in and talked to employers. They asked them, "Would you employ a worker with a disability?" Over 90% of the employers had never been asked. Over 70% said "yes". It was good news - based on much hard work. That project's success generated other ideas. We looked for a business opportunity that could allow house bound individuals to work part or full time. We decided on a telephone answering service. Enormous energy went into setting this up. Like many small businesses, it didn't work. Fortunately, we learned to fail quickly, and we kept on going.

A second spin off was the idea for a conference - one that actually would give people with disabilities an opportunity to speak for themselves. Our working title was "Labelled Disabled", and it turned into a great event, many months later. That event had an enormous impact on many lives, including our own. We met many people who have become friends and critical to our lives as we explored the unknown. One of those fortuitous meetings was with Dr. Doug Biklen, from Syracuse University at a conference about accessible transportation. But all that was to follow...

Marsha was then teaching full time at York. Much to Judith's amazement, as they became friends, Marsha asked Judith to do things for her - like help teach her class. They had lunch together. Actually, Marsha usually ate both lunches. As she helped Judith, she was hungry and absent minded and nibbled more than her share. This eccentric behavior was so fascinating to Judith that she actually wondered if Marsha was a "witch". What did this weird woman really want? Real trust took months to develop. In the meantime, Marsha asked Judith to our home. I built a ramp so she could get in, and Judith began coming regularly. Judith couldn't believe I had actually built a ramp just for her. It didn't seem like a big deal to me. Why wouldn't I build a ramp for a friend? For her, this was a frightening experience - actually being invited to someone's house. We didn't quite understand why it was notable. Judith was a fascinating and interesting woman with an incisive wit. She was pleasant to spend time with. The fact that her visits involved wheelchair transfers and bathroom attendant care (on a mat on the floor or a bed) were not dominant in our thinking.

I had done plenty of attendant care as a university student in Saskatchewan. It wasn't hard. But it is easy to forget that in Judith's experience, most people were frightened away by these normal bodily functions. To many, Judith was a character, a fascinating anecdote, but still too strange to risk being a friend. We didn't see it that way. We just became friends. We shared a common sense of humour, a love of eating (especially Chinese dim sum), and a common vision. Our relationship wasn't charitable; we were working on issues together. Judith was struggling to make York University more accessible and that was a fascinating challenge. And we all worked on the Labelled Disabled planning group.

Judith "Lived" on a Geriatric Ward...

Judith did not push us to visit her "home" on the geriatric ward. In fact, she actively avoided inviting us. It was her way of trying to separate the two worlds - her successful world of work, and her living/dying nightmare. Eventually, it just happened in the normal evolution of events. I remember our first visit. It was devastating. She lived in a hospital ward. It was clean and florescent bright. Institutional warmth oozed nowhere. It was early in the evening, and Judith was in bed. She explained that she had to go to bed whenever the nurses could fit her in. The same went for eating. The agony of her roommate's impatient wait for the peace of death cocooned us in gloom. Judith managed to smile and chatter, but we left mumbling "the gods must be crazy!". She was "living" on a death ward. The psychological abuse was extreme. No one deserved to live like that.

We visited several times. Each was more painful. On one visit, we met Judith's parents. They were an older couple, no longer able to lift and manage Judith's physical needs as they had for the first two decades of her life. They were very pleasant. But on the second or third meeting, they turned to dry ice and asked to meet us privately. They had been visiting Judith, and she had been talking to them about us with great enthusiasm. The conversation was short - and took me years to understand. But I understand it now. "We want you to stop seeing Judith immediately. She has had friends before. They have abandoned her and she has been hurt. Stop seeing her now before you hurt her even more deeply. You too will abandon her. So for her sake, don't cause her any more pain. She has had enough in her life. Good night."

We couldn't believe what we were hearing. We didn't understand it. "But Judith is our friend. What do you mean we shouldn't see her anymore?" "You will abandon her, just like all the rest have. So don't cause her any more pain. Break it off now. Don't hurt her any more." We protested that we wouldn't abandon Judith. I know they didn't believe us. Only now, after many years do we truly understand the depth of their concern.

I had been standing with an orange in my hand. I just remember that my hand was sticky and pulpy. The orange was misshapen. We felt as squeezed as the innocent orange. As we drove home, we realized that we would keep on seeing Judith. She was our friend. We didn't do this to defy Judith's parents. We couldn't even comprehend their directive. We just kept on seeing Judith - and that was the beginning of my learning. Now, in this decade, we all have Christmas or

Thanksgiving dinners together - at her parents'. None of us abandoned each other.

Only now, many years later, do I faintly understand the pain of that first conversation. At the time, I am sure I thought that Judith's parents were awful people. Now, I am amazed that they managed to bring Judith up as a full person, with every conceivable pressure against them. Their reaction was from love and from experience. They had seen Judith approached and abandoned, again and again. They had watched her suffer. They knew they were at their limit. They did what little they could to protect her. It was the only reasonable response. It took me a long time to understand.

Judith never knew about that conversation in West Park until she read these drafts. She knew of others like it, but not that one. We have talked a great deal about how to say it so it didn't sound so tough. We decided to leave it.

You Misinterpreted Us...

Recently, we met with Judith's parents to talk about this story. It was not an easy meeting. They were upset. They felt that although this was the story of the Joshua Committee, it left out the years of struggle that preceded its existence. They were absolutely correct. I made no attempt to write Judith's biography. Perhaps the next project can be the first twenty-five years.

Judith spoke about the fact that only recently had she been able to appreciate the extent of her parents support and sacrifice. However, part of the pain of reading the manuscript was to see some of Judith's inner thinking laid bare. Rita and Ted did everything they could to make Judith a happy child.

She wasn't . They didn't want to hear that. They fought so
hard that they had to believe she was happy. Sometimes the
truth hurts - like in this case. It wasn't a matter for blame, but
that did not reduce the pain.

Ted and Rita added some elements that are integral to this
part of the story.   Firstly, they talked about the battle for
schools. Rita bitterly recalled a superintendant who was very
clear: "We don't want your daughter in our schools." They
moved, and not just once. Ted remembered putting casters on
a desk for Judith at school. They didn't have a wheelchair
when she was small. The schools did nothing. Ted built
ramps everywhere. Ted commented, "That's not in your
story!" The difficulty is that Judith now appreciates what an
incredible accomplishment it was to get her to school. But as
a child, she wanted friends, and to feel part of things. She felt
lonely and left out. Her parents did everything humanly
possible, but they could not make Judith happy. She simply
wasn't. That was hard for them to hear.

Ted and Rita also talked about the breakdown of all the
systems which ultimately placed Judith in West Park. No one
wanted that. They knew that Judith would suffer in that
oppressive kind of environment. But they had run out of
choices, time, energy and money. Ted talked about their
"fail-safe" apartment plan. After eighteen months in a nursing
home following her graduation, Judith and her dad worked on
an arrangement for her to move out with a live-in companion.
They bought an apartment and moved in. All went well for
three weeks until Mrs. Jasperson was nearly killed in a car
accident. After spending a day alone, Judith was rushed into
chronic care, and one month later was "placed" in West Park.
The family was crushed.

As Ted, Rita and Judith reconstructed this forlorn and

buried dream turned nightmare, Rita reminded Judith that there were other complications. Following her back surgery in July, 1972, Judith lost the use of her arms and hands. Although Judith never had full use of her limbs, she had been able to do an enormous amount for herself. The complexity of her attendant care support needs increased dramatically. Ted and Rita could do no more. It was beyond their personal capacity.

Then there was Judith's strong will. Like most teenagers, Judith was unwilling to see the greater wisdom of some of her parents ideas. I gathered by innuendo that the purchase of an apartment might well have been one of those disputes. Rita recalled Judith sitting in their living room and announcing, "You are not going to tell me what to do!" Judith acknowledged that such struggles were true - just like for any other teenagers.

This story is about the origins of the Joshua Committee. There is another story that needs to be told about the first two decades of pioneering work that Judith and her family accomplished. But, it seemed unjust not to pay tribute to Ted and Rita's success in producing a remarkable daughter - Judith Snow.

Now I don't have guilt pangs as I relate the conversation we had with them at West Park. They don't remember it, or even our being there. That doesn't surprise me, or detract from the power of that conversation. They were at wits end. They had endured rejection and abandonment for over twenty years. Naturally they acted to protect their daughter in the only way they knew - with love, strength and determination.

Out of context, they seemed mean. Given history, they were heroes.

Origins of the Joshua Committee

Person - or Terminal Disability...

Just spending time with Judith was a learning experience.
I went to a seminar at Sunnybrook Hospital about that time.
Part of the "show and tell" on disabilities featured slides of
experimental surgery on Judith's back. The medical termi-
nology used to describe my friend skirted the fact that she
used to have limited use of her hands, but that the experiment
failed. Post surgery, Judith's physical existence was con-
strained by total paralysis of her hands - except for 1 inch
movement of her right thumb, and from her chin up. She was
left with full sensation, and a dramatic increase in dependence. The quickness of her mind compensated for much of
the paralysis, (one of the "muscular" diseases from birth).
But most people could not see past the wheelchair - the
disability - to meet this incredible person.

That year, as we grew closer, our mutual frustration with the absurdity of "home" being mutated into "living in a geriatric centre" germinated. Gradually, as trust matured, Judith began to talk about fears she had been unable to admit - even to herself. She had accommodated to "living" at the geriatric centre. She had been there since 1975. Actually she was first placed in the nursing home wing. When their profit margin dipped too low, she was moved to the chronic care - geriatric wing. This was the logical conclusion following her graduation from York University with a Masters degree in psychology. The relentless lobbying of her parents resulted in the first Vocational Rehabilitation Services (VRS) grant to pay for fees and attendant care at the only flat (accessible) university in Canada (York). A fellow student in residence doubled as attendant/roommate. This system worked for seven years, but when Judith graduated, her government grant as a student evaporated. She had already stretched the limits of student support to new horizons. She had no other choice but to move into an institution.

Judith knew the options. She had worked for years with her parents to invent and create programs and projects with attendant care support. Unfortunately, there was still no facility in Ontario that was even remotely able to provide the number of attendant care hours per day that Judith needed to live and work. She was "too needy". Thus, the government's enlightened bureaucratic response was geriatric centres... where she could be "attended to" while waiting for death. For a young woman, it was not a charming future. She had dulled her expectations, and turned up the rose tint. She simply didn't think about it. It would tend to depress one.

Instead, Judith drove the facility crazy. She insisted on going to work every day. No one could quite decide if this was illegal or just annoying. The legal question arose because under Ontario law, if you are disabled, you are by definition unemployable. Ergo, if you are employable, you are not disabled. As ever, Judith didn't fit. She was clearly physically disabled, and she was working as Director of the Centre for Handicapped Students at York University - a position she created - the first of its kind in Canada. Thus, Judith caused discomfort and outrage at her "home" because she broke the rules and the schedules. She wanted to get up before 11:00, have breakfast, and go to work. Their compromise was "choose one" - so Judith went to work. When she returned at the end of the day, she often missed her "feeding" slot. Since the schedule was written on immutable stone tablets, she often missed dinner. As I think back, Marsha eating Judith's lunches may have been a greater sacrifice than we realized, but it was one she never complained about.

The geriatric system's discomfort with this problem patient who wasn't sick deteriorated. Vitamin supplements were added to compensate for missed meals. But no one checked, and the red dye in one of the tablets caused a severe reaction. Judith began to get very ill. She was finally hospitalized at Toronto General in August, 1979. She was diagnosed as having severe malnutrition (from not being fed), and oedema (water retention) caused by not being allowed to go to the bathroom regularly. During those two weeks in hospital, Judith realized that there was no need to be malnourished or bloated. She decided to fight back. She begged them to find an alternate place. She didn't want to return to West Park. But there was no choice. She was returned. In spite of her fighting spirit, her health began to slip again.

When Judith decided to demand "human" service, it was a declaration of war on the institution. They assigned what she termed the "goon squad". Her body was very fragile physically. She could not be moved even slightly without pain. She remained virtually in a sitting position - even in bed. This made Judith a very difficult lift. But the staff assignments were the "tough" nurses. Additionally, virtually all new immigrant staff who spoke little or no English were assigned to Judith, as many as 12-14 different staff per week! This added both strain and pain to Judith's existence. Many staff were under-trained. For survival purposes, Judith became their trainer. Their lack of English meant that her only mode of communication, language, was severely limited. She paid in pain. Supervisors knew but would not change the staffing schedules.

The war of nerves also extended to the pocket book. Judith had been paying $350 per week to have a private nurse get her up in the morning so she could get to work. West Park ruled that private nurses could not be allowed after September, and that Judith would have to be moved to a public ward unless she could pay an additional $350 for a semi-private room. The overlap in the numbers was a re-markable coincidence.

Judith Was Preparing to Die...

It is little wonder that under these circumstances, Judith was preparing to die. She had been told from birth that "people like that" don't survive past 30. She was on the verge. All the signs and symbols were there. The whole world was giving her the same message. They were preparing her for the inevitable.

But as her health deteriorated, the spark that kept Judith

alive would not snuff so easily. She looked for an escape hatch. She wanted a holiday from it all.

In desperation, Judith went to a campus physician who allowed her to move into a university residence for a two-week rest period. She paid her own attendant care with her meager savings. While there, she started seeing a nutritionist who promptly discovered that she was severely allergic to food dyes. All the vitamins she had been taking were dye coated, thus progressively making her sicker. As she changed the pills, the additional drugs to treat the reactions became unnecessary. She began to feel healthier.

Escape From West Park - Oct. 5, 1979...

During those two weeks, she decided that she would never go back to West Park. She knew it would kill her. She would die there. The answer was simply not to go back. If it meant dying in the street, that was better than on a geriatric ward...

Although it wasn't a very good solution, Judith moved into the corridor of a friend's apartment in the student residence at York University. Anything was better than West Park. She thought she only had to manage for five months, since she had been promised a spot in an apartment building with a built in attendant care program.

Her friend, Tracy had some attendant care, so they shared attendants. All of Judith's salary and savings went to pay additional wages for attendants so she could be allowed to work. We only learned how desperate this situation was over time. Judith was so chipper at not being in the geriatric centre that she maintained a stiff (and smiling) upper lip. Even now she recalls holding back from us. She was determined to tough it out on her own. Besides, she was confident that the government's plans for new apartments with attendant care services built in would be the real answer to her needs. She and her mother had helped design them. The announcements were imminent.

Gradually, stress fractures took their toll. Her lend-lease roommate was moving on; the shared attendant care arrangement collapsed at the end of January, 1980 as Tracy moved to one of the apartments Judith had helped design. At the same time, Judith got another letter informing her that there was no room for her at the inn. The student volunteers' enthusiasm and regularity dwindled particularly at exam time, and Judith's cash reserve evaporated. The stress of having to organize people to volunteer or be paid to get you up, on and off the bed pan, fed - to work - back - fed and to bed. It was too much.

None of us really understood the intensity of Judith's survival work load, because we knew her in the context of her job. She wanted to keep us thinking that way. She loved that. We didn't see "the handicap called Judith who also works", but rather a very talented colleague who happens to use a wheelchair and needs someone else's hands to eat, go to the bathroom, get dressed and go to bed.

On the morning of March 6, 1980, she woke up with no one to get her up and dressed. She couldn't even phone anyone for help. She was broke and at the end of her wits.

On March 6, 1980, Judith collapsed.

Judith Collapsed...

On that fateful morning, someone eventually materialized and got Judith up. She drove her chair over to her friend Peter Dill's office. She uttered a few words, "I can't do it any more...". Then Judith stopped talking. For many of us, this might increase the clarity of our communication. For Judith, it meant no communication. She had given up. She just couldn't manage any more. She knew what the system's response would be - reinstitutionalization. Consciously she had decided she would rather die. But in a last desperate flailing for help, she drove to Peter's office. Later, she re-called hoping that Peter would understand she was at wits end. If her friends wanted her to live, they would have to figure it out. She couldn't do it alone any more.

Peter figured that much out. He called Marsha. Marsha called me and a van, and in the afternoon, Judith was trans-ported to our house. Marsha and I made a cosy little recovery room upstairs. I carried Judith up and left her to rest. Shaunee, our yellow labrador had a long standing licking relationship with Judith. They didn't need speech. Shaunee, sensing Judith's trauma, nuzzled in and lick-washed her hands and face. Some people might have been offended. For Judith, it was maternal healing. Just like a dog to do what we humans couldn't.

Meanwhile, we phoned Judith's friends and called an emergency meeting in our living room that night. There were fourteen people. Judith didn't want to come down, or even send a message. It was up to us.

We all had to decide if we wanted Judith in the world - and if so, how we were going to make that happen. Even in a few hours of providing attendant care, we had learned that this was

not a task you just slipped into a busy day. It was a busy day
in its own right. The first decision was self evident. People
had come because they were committed to Judith being in the
world with us. How? What was needed? What would we
do? We were all a bit frantic. But within the group, we
formed natural interest teams to tackle various issues.

* Someone needed to be sure that Judith was talked
back from the brink of suicidal stress. Peter volun-
teered to be the lead person and organize others to
support him.

* Judith would need a place to live. The group
from York University, led by Marsha and Peter,
agreed to pull out all the stops to try and get decent
housing on campus immediately.

* Attendant care translated into dual crises - personnel and money. Several of the group worked out
shifts on the spot to cover the following two weeks.
Peter Dill recruited two of his colleagues from the
National Institute on Mental Retardation (NIMR)
[now the Canadian Association for Community
Living - CACL]. Peter Clutterbuck and I agreed to
intensify our lobbying for money for attendant care.
We were already convinced from this most recent
collapse that a totally voluntary system was stop-gap
at best. Sandy Gray agreed to coordinate the volunteer attendants, in the hope that we would find a
budget before volunteers burned out.

That weekend, in the midst of the chaos, Marsha and I
went to Guelph for a conference. In spite of the crisis, we
were confident that all was in hand, and Judith was secure at
our house. I had forgotten about our leaving. Judith recalled

the tension very quickly. She thought we were abandoning her. She didn't know us well enough to understand that this was normal for us. We weren't abandoning - just busy. We of course had no notion of the extent of Judith's fear of abandonment. We hadn't really understood it at West Park when her parents lectured at us. Judith never mentioned it. How could we have understood? So that weekend, in the midst of a survival crisis, we laid the seeds for the next crisis of confidence. Judith did the only thing she could. She judged us on the basis of a life long experience of abandonment. We didn't even see the problem. It's hard to understand life from someone else's shoes.

Within two weeks, there was a kind of stability in Judith's life. Sandy Gray undertook the round-the-clock coordination of attendant care. Peter and Marsha got the University to allocate a student apartment for Judith. Peter Dill's personal support was bringing Judith back into voice. Peter Clutterbuck and I worked on budgets and proposals. There was movement within the Ministry of Community & Social Services (COMSOC) regarding funding. The problems weren't all solved, but we had begun to learn how to work together. Although we didn't know it yet, the Joshua Committee was at work.

Labelled Disabled - Public or Private - A Strategic Decision...

The Labelled Disabled Conference was scheduled to be a dramatic event. Everyone participated in the Saturday session, including Judith. But the real life drama that was underway made any conference pale in comparison.

Judith's collapse came four days before the opening of the "Labelled Disabled" Conference. It was a three day event. Monday evening (March 10) was the presentation by "consumers" - real people with disabilities speaking their stuff. On Thursday evening there were presentations by agencies - providers of services. Saturday (March 15) was a marathon session to bring all the groups together and hopefully generate new relationships and understandings. Judith had worked hard on the planning and was scheduled to be one of the speakers that first night. She didn't make it. But on the Thursday, we dragged her from the "recovery room" in our house. She appeared pale but was feisty on the stage - where she squared off with an Assistant Deputy Minister from the Ministry of Community and Social Services (Ontario). He had been shuffling Judith's file on and off for 11 years. As part of the conference preparation, several of us had worked with Judith to document her 11 year struggle for independent living. We had a three inch binder of "passing the buck" letters that left almost no senior politician or bureaucrat unscathed. The ADM knew it, and like any good bureaucrat, was paid to avoid embarrassment.

Warner Troyer, a noted CBC television journalist, hosted the panel that crucial night. Live and on video tape, Warner engineered the ADM into a corner. "Will you now promise that Judith Snow will have a place to live - with attendant care? Yes or no! No more waiting. Eleven years is long enough to wait for an answer!" It was a bit of a set up, but cornered, the ADM made the promise. "I guarantee this government will find a place for Miss Snow with attendant care." Troyer was merciless. "Give us a date." Pitt acquiesced. "By May 31." What could he say? It was clear that many of us were tenacious. Given Judith's collapse, we had nothing to lose. He was cornered into a promise.

In the weeks surrounding the conference, a group of us with Judith engaged in an important academic and ethical debate. We were struggled with the dilemma of targeting global legislative change, or individual exceptions as toeholds for policy precedents, (financing Judith's personal attendant care for example). Most of us really wanted to fix the system once and for all (perhaps with a shade of naivete). But the key person in this discussion was Judith. After all, she was the living pioneer. It was fine for us to talk, but it was her life. She also had to decide whether she was willing to use her life as a case history of frustration. How far she was willing to let her life become a public document? Those were hard discussions. There had been a kind of agreement that we would not focus on any individual case. But that was before Judith collapsed. The eventual outcome was that Judith decided she would go public with her life, in order to force the changes required. The Joshua Committee decided that - with Judith.

We all wanted to see legislative change. However, as Judith's life situation daily grew more tenuous, we really had only one choice. We had to get support for Judith - or she would die. Martyrdom can be useful, but it was our considered opinion that we had a better chance to change legislation with Judith feisty and kicking. After all, a five hundred pound "attack wheelchair" isn't something to be trifled with...

We really struggled for the ideal. We assumed it meant more than simply fighting for Judith. But we gave in.   Judith decided she was willing to make her life public. We would fight for her survival first. Months, perhaps years elapsed before we comprehended the strategic impact of our actions. In retrospect, it was the best possible decision, both for Judith and for legislative change. It was an intensely personal issue. This gave both us and the government motivation to move. The action required was relatively small, so even government could risk being creative - under duress. All that is much clearer now. A decade later, we are celebrating the dawn of new legislation that provides personalized mobile attendant care for 500 individuals. As usual, Judith will be the experiment. But it will be a relief to have a policy framework for survival, rather than always squeezing a heartbeat from a collage of funding gimmicks.

It was high drama. For the first time in months, perhaps years, Judith began to believe that she wasn't crazy. It was a real breakthrough for her. Maybe she did deserve to live. Maybe the mythology she had been force fed most of her life wasn't true. Maybe she could live - and be "just" Judith Snow. Ironically, some people could not, or did not want to deal with reality. They instigated rumors that the whole conference had been engineered simply as an "ego trip"—that Judith had actually staged her illness. The whole thing was just an attempt to grab attention. That was annoying, but we couldn't battle rumors. It wasn't possible or useful. We continued on. The truth was much stronger than any invented version.

I don't think any of us realized it then, but that week was the birth of what Judith later dubbed the "Joshua Committee", because we blew down the walls. A group of friends rallied around Judith to protect her life. In so doing, we all discovered the real value of living. Other partnerships were forged at that conference. Until then, all the disability groups operated in isolation and/or antagonism. This wasn't overcome that single night. But that week, the activists from the various networks (who had only heard of each other) suddenly met. It was a seminal event. The alliances that were explored that night cut across disabilities, and led to concerted action on a number of fronts. People who felt they were voices in the disability wilds suddenly had allies. Most of them didn't need much more. They just needed to know they weren't crazy.

The Money Hunt

Waiting for Godot - and Attendant Care Money

The waiting phase was long. Governments need time to
work out procedures. We had no choice but to be patient.
During this phase, Judith was measured, weighed, examined,
scrutinized, and assessed on every known government form,
and by almost every known assessment expert. After the
tenth set of enormously complex forms that required staff
visits and detailed information of the most intimate, personal
and irrelevant nature, we rebelled. We said, "No more".

It was redundant to document once again that in fact Judith
was disabled and needed assistance to brush her teeth, etc.
No. She would not get better. Yes, she would need attendant
care services for the rest of her life.

We decided to propose an end run. Our new strategy was
"lunch therapy". We invited the Minister, the Deputy Minister

and the Assistant Deputy Minister for lunch at Judith's
apartment. We promised we would be frank and answer all
reasonable questions - one more time. We didn't really
expect the Minister, but we did get the ADM. That was
enough. We rehearsed. We had some of Judith's attendants
briefed to talk about our system which was allowing Judith to
be independent. Marsha was to outline the work that Judith
was doing at York and elsewhere - to confirm the legitimacy
of her contribution to society - as if that were needed. Peter
was to explain our support structure around Judith. I was the
"independent administrator" from Frontier College - willing
to be responsible for the grant and all the vital bureaucratic
stuff. We had a good show - with Judith as ring master.

All went according to plan. Our show was flawless.

Then it was time for the ADM to speak. He did - very
briefly. He began reciting some of the social work interview
questions that we had already answered in writing and inter-
views ten times in the past few weeks. It was nearly a fatal
mistake. Peter, a gentle religious person by trade and nature,
suddenly exploded from his pastoral quietude. Hell could not
have generated a more searing inferno. I restrained him
physically as his temples pulsed with rage. "How dare you
ask those questions again! If you are so incompetent to have
come here without being fully briefed, you should resign. If
you are so unethical as to ask them again when you already
know the answers, you are an unprincipled hypocrite, and you
must resign! Get out!" Childhood Sunday School images of
Christ attacking the money lenders flashed to mind.

Needless to say it was tense. Fortunately, it was a very
small apartment. We had planned to have the ADM cornered,

so he could not move. Peter was mortified at his own out-burst and left in moments. I played peacemaker. I explained that Peter's rage was unfortunately justified. We had answered all the questions - ten times in the past few weeks. The official was also mortified. Soothing pleasantries were uttered and everyone crawled back into their cracks.

A post mortem of a nuclear explosion is a little frightening. As we pieced our nerves together, we knew that there were only two possibilities. One was that we had just wiped out any and all future funding for Judith in Ontario. The other was that for all the wrong reasons, it just might break the 11 year log jam. All we could do was wait. The deadline was fast approaching.

It was deathly quiet for the next few weeks. No one said anything to anyone. When COMSOC asked for a delay, we took the opportunity to renew our commitment to Judith. We were very clear. We informed them that Warner Troyer had agreed to host a press conference - the day following our deadline - June 1. **IF** the government provided support as promised, the message would be one of congratulations for innovative leadership. Failure to comply with their own promises (on video) would result in every network news-caster known to Troyer being handed the full 11 year dossier of broken promises. No one, including the premier, would be exempted from buck passing on their own letterheads.

It was at the eleventh hour - in fact 11:30 p.m. on May 31, 1980. I got a call. "Would Frontier College consider taking a contract to manage attendant care support for Judith Snow?" I agreed. There was a condition. We weren't to tell anyone. It was a unique arrangement - the first Order in Council (on the continent as it turned out) to provide attendant care services to an individual. [An OIC is a special finance "bill" passed

42

by the cabinet to respond to issues that are not covered by existing legislation.] The government was concerned it would be seen as a precedent and they would be overwhelmed by applications.

That first contract was a policy breakthrough. It was for six months only, retroactive to April 1st, until Oct. 1, 1980. It was conditional on York University setting up an Attendant Care Project to assist students with disabilities. It provided money for 5 hours of attendant care per day. But with all the restrictions, it was a major victory and we celebrated.

Needless to say, the news leaked out, at our press conference! Over time, the government of Ontario was plagued with about 140 Order In Council grants. It wasn't the tide they were frightened of, but it was enough to create the pressure to begin legislative change. But all that was to come much later. The short story is that it worked. It wasn't perfect. The government still will not allow funds for attendant care to be paid directly to an individual. Regardless of details, it was a massive victory. Judith was alive and about to begin life anew - as a citizen, not as a body awaiting rigor mortis in a decorated mortuary. Our strategic choice to support Judith first, and seek full legislative action later, turned out to be the correct strategy, even though we had backed into it reluctantly. Never argue with success..

Meanwhile, as the money lobby continued, we had to design/invent a workable attendant care model, and translate it into bureaucratic language. The translation was the easy part. Agreeing was not. We all reverted to our chosen careers. Peter Dill argued persuasively (not to me) that attendant care should be "spiritual" and "voluntary". Another felt this was a feminist issue. Some of us argued that this was work and thus money was required to pay people. It seems

43

hard to believe now, but we debated heatedly about the role of volunteerism in Judith's attendant care.

And Then The Flower Child Blossomed...

We were just beginning to comprehend the complexity of Judith's daily struggle for survival. The fact that others were taking a serious interest allowed her to relax a little for the first time in many months. Part of the relaxation was to do some social experimentation. She simply had not been able to fit it in to the constant crisis of recent years. I dubbed this period Judith's "hippie" phase. She developed all the characteristics of a genuine flower child. And why not? But as one of the "nose to the grindstone" types in our group, I got very antsy when Judith started talking about "not working for a year or so", and "moving downtown." I could hardly believe it. For the first time in months, Judith had an apartment, attendant care and a job. The structure was far from shatterproof. But Judith started talking about change. My reaction was that the last thing Judith needed to do was screw up the only working system we had - by becoming a "flower child". And I suspect I had a touch of the ungrateful virus. How could she even think that, after all we have done.

That was one of the times I learned. I had to learn to listen - and to respect the rights of an individual. I don't mean that I didn't tell Judith that I thought "dropping out" was ridiculous. I advised very bluntly that I thought moving from the university to downtown Toronto was very risky. I didn't soften my opinion because Judith was in a wheelchair. She was an adult. I likely told her she should behave like one. (Actually, as Judith read this, she corrected me. She was crystal clear that I did tell her, not once, but several times. Now it comes back to haunt me.) Fortunately, Judith prevailed. Others talked to me too. It was Judith's life. We could and should make our opinions known, but she would decide. We were there to support her right to decide. And decide she did. She moved.

Crisis or Opportunity?

The October 1st deadline arrived. York University had decided there would be no Attendant Care Project at York. Judith had decided that she no longer wanted to direct the Centre there. She gave up her job. She applied to law school. Although accepted, she decided not to go. Thus, by fall, Judith had no contract for attendant care, no job, no student status. Crisis was a word that leapt to mind.

Fortunately, the ADM who had rammed through the first Order in Council (after lunch therapy) decided to give us a one year extension until October, 1981. Then Judith went to work and cashed in a few more "chips". She got a Scottish Rite Bursary, and arranged a few teaching contracts at York and with Program Analysis of Service Systems (PASS) workshops. It wasn't a lot, but it was enough to give us a semblance of security. We survived 1981.

Months later, we learned that the ADM we had met had retired shortly after granting Judith's extended contract. Several corroborated the story. This man was devastated by the meeting. He had forgotten that there were real people at the end of the paper trail. He told several colleagues that when he began his career, it was because he wanted to help people. Judith's meeting reminded him of his neglected and sidetracked commitment to genuine service. As his final act in the bureaucracy, he rammed through an Order in Council for Judith Snow. Then he retired.

One of the lessons for all of us is to remember that there are very fine people buried in the bowels of all bureaucracies. We have to get to their hearts, not their policy manuals.

It Wasn't All Fun..

For months after the second Order in Council was approved in October, there was no money. Frontier College fronted cash to pay attendants while this new procedure was worked out. It took almost a year. During that time, we learned a great deal about the nature of attendant care. Initially, we all thought of attendant care as charitable work - Judith included. That meant that we looked for people to donate time, and occasionally, we would try to offset their expenses with a bit of remuneration. We were definitely in the charity mode. This meant Judith had to be charitable to everyone. Sometimes when you want a cup of tea or simply to go to the bathroom, you don't feel like chatting. Sometimes you just want peace. Charitable volunteers of course expected to be thanked for their service with constant appreciation and smiles. It's hard to be appreciative when you are trying to train someone to lift you properly, they aren't listening, and it hurts. The expectations were contradictory. We began to understand the complexity of attendant care.

The constant financial crisis loomed. Judith couldn't survive with only five hours of paid attendant care . We had exhausted all the obvious sources. Clutterbuck invented a lateral move. He found a grant that would pay for drivers.

Our adaptation was "attendant-drivers" and we managed to get some extra help that way for two years.

We also learned about scheduling. Judith had been doing it for so long that almost no one realized the enormity of the task. As we all variously tried and screwed up, we again learned that this was no trivial task. We began to explore having a paid attendant care coordinator.

And then, as people made the slow transition from charitable voluntarism, to semi-paid employment, all the complexities of staffing emerged, with all the wrinkles that human beings bring with them. We learned a great deal. Much later, we rearranged our mental picture again. We transformed Judith from a "charitable activity", to Judith - "Job Creation Project" and employer. After all, Judith was creating approximately three full time jobs - and they were excellent jobs. They were apprenticeships to life on the edge. Almost no one who tried it regretted the learning. When we changed our thinking to seeing the attendant care jobs as an alternative graduate course and a good job, it was much easier to hire (and fire) appropriate employees. It was no longer a personal charitable sacrifice. It was a job. We could insist on standards of performance. It reduced the stress substantially. Of course, it never ends because Judith needs someone to assist her all the time. That is the fact. It will never change. It was very hard for all of us to come to terms with that fact that Judith's life would always be a crisis.

Through it all, life improved. Judith's skin took on new colour - from actually eating regular, fresh, home-made meals. She began to explore various consulting contracts as the Centre for Handicapped Students at York finally receded into her past. The transition wasn't so traumatic. Even I was forced to admit it.

Accidents Will Happen...

When we first knew Judith, she depended almost entirely on "Wheeltrans" for her transportation. If any of you have experienced this, you will understand that this bus/taxi service is not a service. It runs your life. Thus, when given the opportunity to invest in a rusting jalopy with a swing hoist that was bolted on the roof, Judith leapt at the chance. It was miserable to work. The car was temperamental at best, and unreliable. But when it went, you could decide where and when you wanted to go and that was spectacular. Safety was another issue. Getting Judith in and out of the car was not a minor accomplishment. It was an acquired skill. As each person acquired it, Judith paid in pain. And even once learned, you could still screw up. I did.

The first time I sprained Judith's ankle was on her first visit to our house. She wanted to see the upstairs. I picked her up and in my arms, we toured the 2nd story. However, I stretched my limits. Coming down the stair I was tiring and bounced her head on a post - no damage. Then, exhausted, I virtually dropped her in her wheelchair - and sprained her ankle. Great start. As Judith helped me to remember this (my memory was selectively foggy), she reflected on how much pain has shaped her life. For years, every move caused agony. That definitely alters a person's outlook. It may even have slowed the growth of our friendship, since I inflicted pain that hurt both of us.

Undaunted, I tried again. My next catastrophe was a step up from a sprained ankle. I broke it. Judith's that is. We were rushing to her 30th birthday party. I was rushing. We were all rushing. I didn't listen. I pushed/dropped Judith into her chair and tried to swing her feet around in one quick motion. It should have worked. But it didn't. Judith shrieked in pain. I had caught her shoe on the wheelchair foot-plate. When I turned, I broke her ankle. Her pain continued throughout the pizza party near York University. She never let it interfere with a good time.

However, the next day, she went to the hospital for x-rays. Broken ankle. What a shmuck. I felt like crap. But Judith never held a grudge. She was more worried that it would stop me from lifting her. Getting around was much more important than a broken ankle. Not everybody in a wheelchair gets their attendant to break their ankle. I took a lot of ribbing. Judith absorbed a lot of pain. She never complained.

Later she acquired a used van with a side lift that functioned most of the time. More recently, her new blue monster is beginning to seem like one of the earlier relics. But who has $40,000 to replace a van and its lift?

Another winter day we were returning from a protest at City Hall. It was cold, sleeting and miserable. Judith was bundled in wraps and covered in plastic as she drove her wheelchair up University Avenue, because there were missing curb cuts in the area. The racing traffic was creating an ice fog, so it seemed very strange when Judith turned and began to drive across the street in the middle of the cars. I ran after her uncomprehending. Then I heard her screaming, "My thumb is frozen...". That might not mean much to you, but Judith drives her wheelchair with her thumb. The freezing rain had frozen her thumb on the contact points and she was totally out of control. We grabbed her chair and steered her back to safety and warmth.

No one ever said driving an electric wheelchair was so exciting.

The Christmas Crisis...

All had been going really well. Judith was a regular at our house. We went out for Chinese food a lot. Then came Christmas, 1980. We had planned to spend Christmas Eve together at our place, stay over, and then on Christmas Day, go to Judith's parents place. We were sitting by the tree, the fire was crackling, our yellow labrador was "washing" Judith's hands and feet. It was perfect. In the excitement of the moment, I mentioned that Marsha and I had just confirmed plans to go to Mexico for three weeks in February with two other friends. The atmosphere was instantaneously trans-formed from glee to gloom. Judith lamented: "You mean you won't be here to hear Dr. Wolfensberger? (Dr. Wolfensberger is a professor and author of <u>Normalization</u>, a book on institutionalization). He's coming to speak. He's is going to visit with me. I'm counting on you to be there with me."

I didn't understand the crisis and said so. "We'll hear him another time." It was the wrong thing to have said. Whining, temper tantrum, sulk - she covered all the bases. Mainly, Judith knew she wouldn't get far with me, so she focused on Marsha. "You never do anything I want to do. You don't care about me... If you really cared, you wouldn't go..." It sounded like a bad movie script - but it was live in our living room - and Judith wouldn't stop. Eventually we simply announced, "We are going to Mexico, and right now, we are going to bed." Judith closed her mouth in a sulk. I put her to bed. Great Christmas Eve.

In the privacy of our room, Marsha & I reviewed our options and decided that this was ridiculous. Judith was behaving like a child - a spoiled child and a brat - and by morning she would be fine.

Morning came. Christmas morning. We all hoped secretly that last night had been a bad dream. But when I went to get Judith up, the only sounds were subdued mumbles. Great! I muddled getting ready for breakfast. Marsha waited to come down - hoping that the nightmare would have passed. When she arrived in the kitchen, Judith spoke. "You're no friend. If you cared about me, you would stay. You're just a selfish..." That was when I interrupted. I hadn't planned it. I just exploded. "If that is how you treat Marsha, you can get the hell out of here! Either be nice - or leave. Take your pick!" The plates on the rack were rattling from decibel concussion. Marsha was stunned and sobbing. Judith turned pale, and in angry disbelief,

"You'd put me in the snow?"

"Are you going to apologize?"

"No!"

"Then I'm throwing you out. Where do you want to go?"

"My parents!"

"Fine."

We phoned ahead and with virtually no explanation said that we would be dropping Judith within the hour. I loaded her in the car and dropped her off.

We didn't talk to Judith till after we got back from Mexico. It was really strange. But then, with the first thaw of spring, we found excuses to explore innocuous topics. Soon we were back up to speed. But now it was different. We all learned a hard lesson. We all learned about dependency - and how destructive it can become - even with the best of intentions. And we all learned about respect for each other as adults. "Life by guilt" isn't much of a foundation. We conquered it the hard way.

Judith graduated from her teen tantrum phase, and we learned to be more careful about creating expectations that cannot be fulfilled. We never talked about this or analyzed it in depth. We just went forward. We all learned a good hard and valuable lesson in the reality of friendship. Friendship isn't all fair weather. This was a hard time. We got through it.

On July 1st, 1990, Marsha, Judith and I reviewed this draft between bites of dim sum at the Kowloon Restaurant, one of our favourites. We agreed that we all should have talked it out that day. But then we backed off. There was no way that we could have understood our divergent perspectives. Judith was focused on abandonment. Every act by every close person was evaluated in terms of potential for abandonment. We scored very high, without knowing. Judith had been unwilling and/or unable to tell us. And we measured the depth of dependency. We were all exploring friendship, but it doesn't happen overnight. It takes time. We needed more time. Fortunately for all of us, we got it. We took it.

Judith Moved Downtown...

We had all helped to move Judith into a regular high rise apartment on St. George Street - near the University of Toronto. Judith was in ecstasy. A regular apartment - just like everyone else. And with the curb cuts in the area, she could go for walks and shopping, and stroll down Yonge street if she wanted. As we watched Judith effervesce, we all appreciated the glory of the ordinary things that make life glow.

During the first week of September, 1981, from her new apartment, Judith glowed on the TV Ontario cameras for a special program for the United Nations International Year for Disabled Persons. Judith was being featured for one half hour segment. Their shoot coincided with our struggle to figure out a better way to manage attendant care. We called together nearly 50 people and spent several hours thinking together. That was when we actually decided that Judith needed the equivalent of three full time positions. Such a simple thought made planning, operating and even fund raising clearer, although not much easier.

Lunch Time Again - Another ADM...

Time passed. Our understanding of the meaning of flexible responsive attendant care deepened. We learned that it was work, and that work costs money. Gradually we shifted our concept from charity to employment generation. We also learned that attendant care costs a great deal - more than we had in the account. We decided to look for more.

We did private fund raising. Everyone said it wouldn't work. We raised $6000 in private donations. That got us through the second financial crisis - and into the next. That was when we decided to go for another government precedent.

I had been working with a very progressive Assistant Deputy Minister, Art Daniels. Remarkably, he had just been transfered to COMSOC. At the beginning of his first week, I booked him for lunch. I knew he loved to eat. I didn't tell him where or what the subject. I didn't want him "briefed" or canceled by his staff. I arrived a few minutes early. Art asked where we were going and what I wanted. He knew that lunches were not just to eat. "We're going to Judith Snow's apartment. I want you to meet her." Art had already heard of

53

Judith in spite of our precautions. Being both creative and quick, he grabbed two of his senior staff to join us. I phoned to say "Two more for lunch".

Judith's new downtown apartment on St. George wasn't far. I gossiped about other topics until we arrived. We sat Art next to Judith and served lunch. He was conveniently positioned so he had to help her eat. His staff were in trauma. One doesn't treat an Assistant Deputy Minister like that. We made our presentation between bites. We congratulated the Ministry on their far sighted policy that allowed for Judith's attendant care to date. Then we explained that it was not enough. Attempted interruptions by staff were cut short by Art. He was fascinated by Judith. She waxed eloquent on the potential for flexible attendant care services that could deinstitutionalize people and make them productive citizens, rather than just expensive wards of the state. Art asked Judith if she would be willing to help the Ministry think about this kind of problem. She just about leapt out of her chair. "I think we should have Judith do some consulting for us, don't you?" Art turned to his staff. They were turning white and it wasn't the lunch. They were also just learning about their new boss. As good bureaucrats, they said, "Yes sir!"

Even over lunch, the COMSOC bureaucrats injected Art with briefing "notes". Judith was the highest cost Order in Council in the province. It was unlikely that her money could be increased. When Art suggested a consulting contract, blood pressures peaked.

In the weeks that followed our August lunch, we had more meetings with Art - in his office. His staff laid down every barrier, and Art simply said, "hire that woman". We agreed that she would give advice to the ministry, and that in fact, the money would go to pay for attendant care. We drew up a contract which had dual and contradictory clauses to cover both parties. For the governments protection, it talked about consulting services; and to protect Frontier College, it acknowledged that the funds would be used to pay for attendant care for Judith Snow. It was for 18 months, to regularize it with other government contracts. Both Art and Frontier College managed to keep that contract from close scrutiny for several years. After Art moved on, one of the many systematic reviews finally found it and hemorrhaged. But by then, the precedent had been in place for several years, and they were forced to simply merge the two contracts into one. Art was smart. He knew that if he had done the logical thing right at the beginning, it would have been killed. By creating a second alternative and separate routing for money, he gave us survival funding for a more flexible attendant care system that was well on the way to creating a whole new government policy. Art knew it. He smiled and turned the other cheek. So did we.

And who says there aren't good bureaucrats. Art Daniels helped us to take another critical step. We owe him a major vote of thanks.

The Funding Search Continued...and Continued...

Our money search was never ending.

From 1982-86, we lived on "Section 38" grants. This was a Manpower Retraining Program for people receiving Unemployment Insurance Commission (U.I.C.) payments. We managed to convince the appropriate federal officials that this was excellent training (which it was), and had enormous success with several attendant workers. There was an inevitable hitch. Frontier College already had numerous Section 38 grants (too many), so the application had to come from the National Institute on Mental Retardation. Jacques Pelletier, the Director, smiled and blessed the lateral dance. But we all knew it could not last.

Art Daniels didn't forget us. He quietly listened for opportunities. About 1985, I received an invitation (at Art's suggestion) to a meeting about a new COMSOC funding program - the Social Service Employment Program (SSEP). I dutifully went and found myself in the COMSOC basement with COMSOC employees from virtually every major institution in the province. I was definitely the only outsider. As the briefing progressed, I was even more confused. The program being outlined was for government agencies to apply for one year salaries to train individuals in their institutions to be job ready. The intent was that participants would move out into full employment. I waited patiently. I was quiet since I doubted that Art's call was an accident, but I could not see the path. When most people had left, I approached the presenter. He knew who I was and suggested we should go for a coffee. In a quiet corner, he asked if Frontier College could make use of the program. I said I would love to, but if the program was for government agencies, I didn't think we qualified. Will Drake smiled knowingly, checked for eavesdroppers, and then enquired further.

"Mr. Daniels informed me that Frontier College has a contract for a Ms. Snow."

"Yes?" I affirmed, searching for the connection.

"In his mind, that makes Frontier College a government agency."

"You mean that Ms. Snow would be eligible to apply for one of these training grants?"

"Definitely," said Mr. Drake.

My eyes were popping. I wanted to check what I thought he was implying...

"And since Frontier College is a government agency for the purposes of this program, its other programs would also be able to apply to the program."

"Yes, I certainly believe so."

Drake was grinning mischievously. I was incredulous. Here was a man standing in front of me saying he would pay grants for full salaries for trainees - perhaps several times over. I love gift horses, but I still check the teeth.

"Would you mind clarifying the process for decisions on this program?"

"I am the process!" Drake replied. "If you get this single page in on Monday, you will have an answer by Friday." It wasn't appropriate to hug a bureaucrat in blue pin stripes, but this man knew his creases were in serious danger. He winked.

"Art thought we should have a little creativity in the program somewhere. You're it."

And so began Art Daniels' second gift to Frontier College and Judith. Both benefited enormously. That tiny opening became the largest single funding source for Frontier College over the next five years. Judith began with one worker. Very quickly, Frontier got in the act. At one time, Frontier College had over 20 full time "trainees" on salary. Ironically, Judith's hunt for money was the key to Frontier's financial survival for the next several years.

Will Drake died of cancer the following year. Fortunately, he had consciously put enough memos in the file that the creative genius that he and Art Daniels had the courage to initiate, was well established. Once again, we found the people who make minor miracles into life saving devices - for Judith and literally hundreds of others. I also like to think of that remarkable success as a living memorial to Will Drake.

Life:
The Good
and
The Other

Judith Stayed for Our Honeymoon...

You certainly don't plan things like that. After living
together for several years, more married than the state could
ever make us, Marsha and I decided to get married formally.
It seemed like a good idea at the time. We had both been
married before. We were both scared, but confident that this
time we had found the real soul-mate of our lives. A friend
of mine summed it up after meeting Marsha, "Pearpoint, this
time you've met your match!" I agreed.

Our wedding was a great day. Fourteen intimate friends
gathered in our living room in a circle. We had asked each
person to be prepared to contribute something special to the

service - whatever they felt was appropriate. It was a bit like a Quaker service. Neil Webster was the master of the ceremony - which he began with his contribution - a beautiful segment of a Wagner choral. My sister, a budding studying actress, who had just finished playing "Dorothy" from the Wizard of Oz, wrote and read a play about the brick road that brought a boy from Shaunavon, Sask., and a girl from New York City together. And she sang. Judith presented us with two gifts. One was a crocheted picture "Thome Sweet Thome", and a small clay mask that she had made - with her own hands - before the surgeons took away the use of her hands. It hangs on our wall - a reminder of our mortality. John O'Leary read selections from Jean Vanier and the Bible. Gus and Maria brought home made Greek food. Henry gave us an album for the photos he took that day. Marlene had decorated our house with arrangements of flowers; Wayne, Ethel - everyone contributed. Marsha read a long poem - her vows to me - which included an endless supply of bran muffins. I told a story. Some things don't change.

All this is a preliminary to how Judith stayed for our honeymoon. By the time the guests had left, it was late. Judith's attendants were exhausted, and the thought of bundling her up for winter travel, the car trip - then getting ready for bed...it was at least another two hours. So we decided she should stay. I am sure she was delighted in a perverse kind of way. We opened the sofa bed, snuggled Judith in for our honeymoon, and retreated to our bedroom upstairs. It was snowing and beautiful in more ways than one.

Just Friends...In Georgia...

   Somewhere not too long after we had done battle with
Judith for her life, she dubbed us the "Joshua Committee" -
for blowing down the walls of theworld so she could get in.
At first I felt a little uncomfortable with naming us, and I
think I squirmed visibly for many months when Judith
referred to her Joshua Committee. But over time I learned
that Judith was prophetic. We were indeed her Joshua
Committee. Gradually, instead of being uncomfortable, I
became proud of being part of this little group. And the little
group became part of me and my life and my work. Now I
can see that I had a self imposed limit for personal involve-
ment. I was there, participating, functioning - just as active as
anyone. But I had an internal protective fuse that stopped me
from getting too close - so I didn't get burned. Judith is very
similar in her own way.   Somewhere on the Georgia trip, I
realized that this friendship was something very special. It
was extraordinary. I decided to let my self believe. That was
when I consciously became part of the Joshua Committee.
Funny how some of us are so slow.
   About that time, John O'Brien and Connie Lyle O'Brien
began to appear in my life. They were from Atlanta, Georgia,
and were spending their lives helping people and
organizations to think about how people might live together
better. They had a two person organization, Responsive
Systems Associates, with a marvellous motto - "No pit too
deep!" Somewhere in his wanderings, John met Judith, and
thus, the Joshua Committee. John was brilliant and quickly
saw the sparkle of something special in Judith - and our
group. In time, he arranged for us to be invited to Georgia, to
go on tour.

The third week of June, 1982 was was an amazing week. Marsha and I, Christa (Judith's attendant) and Judith, all travelling in a dilapidated van with a welded wheelchair lift. We felt like a rock group on tour. We did talks all over - Atlanta, Augusta, Savannah. I freckled brown, except when I careened to a halt in a rural intersection - then I turned white. We exchanged paint with another truck that cut us off as he turned left. Judith's safety belt held firm or she could have faced off with the wind shield. Fortunately, the one strong point of the rental van was its brakes. In between engagements, we ate crab, smoked ribs, and shoo fly pie. Judith had never been in the Atlantic ocean, so I drove her in - wheelchair and all - till the surf nearly dragged us away. In hotel pools, we took Judith swimming. We met wonderful people who worked with Georgia Advocacy - Tom Kohler and his team.

The Southern hospitality was of legendary proportions. We had a wonderful time. Strangely, I don't recall much of the content of our talks. I know we were telling "Judith's story" - the struggle and the pain - the battle for attendant care. I presume we concluded that the struggle was continuing. If we didn't, we were wrong. But, while the details of the tour fade with age, one or more of us is reminded from time to time of the impact of our trip. Apparently it was a critical event for many people in taking another step in their own struggles. There is great clarity about what made the impact. It wasn't the brilliance of any of our talks. It was simply the "image of three friends".

I have been reminded of that several times. What could possibly be so special about three people - friends - giving talks together. But I have been told many times it wasn't the talks. It was us being together. What people had not seen, or seen so seldom, was real friendship that superseded disability. We argued, agreed, disagreed, joked, laughed, travelled, ate, swam, wandered, toured, got grouchy, went for walks - like friends do - together and alone. So our words for all their wisdom were lost on most of the audiences. But they got the message even more powerfully. They watched us being friends. That was the uncommon truth that registered with people for years after our trip. For a person who spends a large portion of life talking and writing, this is a bit disconcerting. But in another way, it is never really what we say that matters; it's what we do, and who we are. And in Georgia, we were "just friends".

And Then We Went Canoeing...

Judith was always one to try everything. She had often joked that she wanted to try canoeing - perhaps because Marsha and I did it and she wanted to test it out. My response to these kinds of requests was always, "No problem!" We had long since decided that accessibility was a state of mind. If Judith wanted to go canoeing, we would figure out a way.

I'm not sure if I really thought that Judith was serious, but over time, I realized she was. The opportunity came when we were all taking the PASS Normalization training workshop from John O'Brien in Kingston. Somehow, we made time.

I didn't even have to bring my canoe because Tony McGilvary had a big one and he thought this was a great idea. Tony was another person who was committed to unlimited possibilities. We arranged to meet at the bridge by Mud Lake. Judith had changed wheelchairs during the interval, so her back support/seat was portable. Basically all we did was place her in the canoe surrounded and knotted to multiple life preservers with the backrest braced against the thwart. Judith was as stable as the canoe.

With Judith suffering a severe attack of glee, we paddled off down the lake. Laurence and I took her out for the first round. When we tired and returned, Judith wanted more, and Tony insisted. Tony's health was already in disastrous shape, but being super macho, he was not about to cave in to any such conventions. Tony took the stern and we paddled off again. I remember it well because Tony didn't paddle very long before his lungs gave out. It took quite a while, but Judith didn't mind and we eventually reentered the reeds where we had started.

It wasn't intentional. I was tired. We were riding very low in the water. As I felt the bow scrape the bottom, I jumped out. It was a classical canoe sinking. Tony weighed in at over 350, so when I stepped out, the bow shot out of the water. Tony panicked. Judith assumed she was going to drown on her first canoe trip. I was no help at all. I was convulsed with laughter. I could see that the stern of the canoe was solidly on the bottom, and the canoe was stable. It was just filling with water. And for a few seconds, Tony was scrambling for his life and Judith's. He was trying to run up-hill in a sinking canoe. Tony couldn't walk five steps let alone run. The sight was a slow motion comedy. Within five seconds - or a life time depending on your perspective - everyone realized that the canoe was sitting solidly on the bottom. Tony was sitting in water panting, and Judith was soaked to the depth of a couple of inches.

In retrospect, I think it was the best possible canoe trip. A safe sinking had real drama. We laughed and I still chuckle when I see their faces. As Judith read this, she commented, "It's a good thing I didn't panic." I didn't grace her denial with a rebuttal. I remember. I was there.

The Integration Action Group...

It all began with a one week course at the Canadian Association for Community Living (formerly the National Institute on Mental Retardation) in the spring of 1984. Marsha was the Visiting Scholar at the Institute and together with Judith they designed a course to assist parents to cope with the challenges and opportunities of children with disabilities.

It was another first and attracted the most amazing group of people. Remarkable as they were, the follow-up was staggering. They decided to keep on meeting. It was a smaller core group, but they decided that someone had to take leadership in advocating for action on integration. They would do it. They struggled with their mandate. It was advocacy for integration. Nothing more and nothing less. They decided not to invest time in arguing with those who disagreed, but rather to advocate and act to promote integration - in schools and beyond.

Seven years later, there are dozens of tiny "Integration Action Groups" in communities across the continent. They don't have budgets. They don't have programs. They do have committed parents who make things happen for integration. They are committed to action.

Seven years later Marsha and Judith are advisors to the board of the original group. They are the "parents" who had the courage to let go. They continue to have a wonderful loving relationship with the growing organization that has emerged from the growing pains of teenhood into the mature strength and conviction of adult life.

It's just another tiny example of the profound effect of a person who "couldn't do anything" because she was in a wheelchair. And of course, she "couldn't do anything" because she was supposed to die when she was thirty.

Accessibility is a State of Mind...

Shortly after that Judith and Laurence Hunt announced their engagement. We had a party and were all anxious to do something special to mark the occasion. There was a ground swell of support to go dancing at the "Diamond Club". Since Saturday night clubbing in Toronto was not my field of expertise, we all raced off with enthusiasm. The lineup was intimidating - but not nearly as frightening as the three full flights of nearly vertical steps. But everyone had decided it was the Diamond Club or bust, so we persisted. We brought Judith's ramps and lots of rope. We estimated that we could pull Judith AND the ramps up each of the three flights as a unit. A fresh challenge.

People were astounded. So were we. It was a crazy notion. But in the process of checking out the stairs, we encountered the fleet of Saturday night bouncers. They might all have been on loan from either body building schools or biker gangs. They were not small. For whatever reason, the notion of Judith dancing was beyond their ken, so they decided to get her in. It was really easy. We were just about to begin the first set of steps when they materialized in formation. They picked up Judith, the chair, and the ramps as if they were styrofoam and marched up three flights of stairs. It was easy.

We had a great time dancing. It was smoky, with strobe lights and sound that resonated in your disks. Judith was nearly picked up by one of the hundreds of strange people that seemed to lurk in the shadows. A good time was had by all.

Leaving was just as easy. We just mentioned that we wanted to go. Judith's body guards hoisted her down the stairs. "Nothing to it. You guys come anytime!" We haven't been back, but it was a symbolic evening. You really can go anywhere if you make up your mind - and ask for help!

From Behind the Piano...

Very recently, Judith told several of us a very personal story - that she had partly buried, and partly denied. It was too painful to remember. But it is such an incredible allegory that it must be told.

The background includes some facts that Judith had told us long before. Her voice is very distinctive - husky - bass. She went from soprano to bass overnight when she was 10 years old. Doctors gave her steroids, experimentally, to see if it would increase muscle strength. One result was wrecked throat muscles and early puberty. Another was that Judith stopped singing and talking. She was embarrassed by the depth of her voice. At age 13, she had two radiation treatments, for the purpose of sterilization. They didn't work. They nearly killed her. There was no justification that makes any sense today. But it was the medical wisdom of the day that "people like that" should be sterilized. They did it to Judith.

A second tragedy was that this trauma fundamentally

undermined Judith's relationship with her family. "How could they do this to me? They wouldn't do it if they loved me..." It set a tone that took decades to overcome.

The story Judith just now recalled, happened in her graduating year in high school. She had regained some confidence and delighted in singing. It was one of the few activities she could participate in fully. When her voice had changed dramatically, children had made fun of her. It was hard for a child to be a bass. But Judith being Judith, she recovered her courage and sang in the school choir anyway. Although the high school welcomed her, Judith's memories are of lonliness. That is why it was so important when the music teacher seemed to like her, and welcomed her participation.

The Christmas concert was approaching. The choir was being featured. Dress rehearsal. Everyone was excited. But during the practice, Judith's favourite teacher "repositioned her" - behind the piano.

She went home and sat in stunned silence. She couldn't cry because it was not acceptable in her family. Her favourite teacher didn't want her either. She was distraught. She didn't know what to do. She desperately wanted to sing, to be part of the concert. She wanted to confront her teacher. But she was afraid that if she did, she would be rejected even more.

The following evening, Judith went to the concert. She placed herself BEHIND THE PIANO and sang. But she stopped singing after that.

We have musical parties at our house. Judith always sits in front of the piano and sings her heart out. We didn't realize how important it was for Judith to sing or to sit in front of the piano. We didn't realize it until just now.

Judith now realizes what a profound experience that was. It was the beginning of Judith choosing to be "handicapped" and live with it. She could have driven in front of the piano, or beside the piano, but she acquiesced. She parked behind the piano of life. She accepted her "station". She chose not to confront her teacher. He likely had no idea about the trauma he was inflicting. But Judith chose to stay quiet. She was 18 years old.

Today of course, Judith has learned that if she stays behind the piano, she is dead. The piano was the nursing home and the geriatric centre. The piano is accepting what "others" decide is good enough for you. So today, Judith is struggling to overcome the traumas suffered by an impressionable teenager, being tucked behind the piano. It was her first concrete memory of being "disabled" and "accepting it". Accepting it was the devestating part.

Reflecting on those unhappy teen years, Judith now knows that was when she was learning "how to be handicapped". She was stubborn. She fought hard. But once learned, "un-learning handicapism" is a formidable challenge. Judith has done it. It is a remarkable feat of endurance and courage.

If Judith, a fighter for life, was trapped into acceptance for nearly 30 years, it is only reasonable to expect that all of us, with a fraction of Judith's determination, have equally accepted externally imposed limits - our own private "piano's" which we hide behind. Once again, her pioneering spirit offers all of us the opportunity to live and learn with her - about our capacity to be free - our capacity to celebrate life - if we will only choose to live.

And Then There Was Surgery

After Twelve years, You Don't Notice the Pain - So Much...

In January, 1988, Judith's health really took a turn for the worse. She had been in pain since 1972. There was no mobility in her hips or joints. There was no muscular tension to hold her limbs in position. Thus, any movement required very careful handling by the attendant, and the grinding of Judith's teeth to offset the pain. It had been like that since her back and hip surgery.

Throughout the fall of 87, movement became agonizing. Judith was both weak and sick a great deal. We had already secured a good family doctor in Yves Talbot, with whom we had founded the University of Toronto Medical School course "Vive la Difference". He was very sensitive to Judith, but quickly referred her to a friendly orthopaedic surgeon since he suspected that the origin of the trouble was to do with her hip surgery.

Judith was terrified of hospitals and doctors. She had been an "experiment" too many times. She was acutely aware that hospitals immediately saw her physical reality as a sickness. It blinded them to her flu or other disease which they could treat. Going to the hospital was very dangerous for Judith. I was chosen to accompany her.

In preparation, we acquired Judith's old x-rays. It was exceedingly strange that all her x-rays, except the immediate pre-surgery plates, were on file. The pile was four inches of x-rays thick. She talked through them as a briefing for me. Judith knew an enormous amount about back surgery (having had it several times). She was a great teacher. One of her theories regarding the increase in pain was that the Harrington Rod (a stainless steel rod running for about 16" along her spine) had slipped - and was thus putting pressure on the base of her spine. We studied the shots of the rods from various angles over the years. Sometimes, we were convinced it was on the move.

The shots of Judith's hips were unique. When the rod was installed, they fused almost all her spinal disks, save five. To do this, a large volume of extra bone was required. The standard procedure is to take a vertical slice from the femur (thigh bone) which is sufficiently thick that normal functioning can be maintained. However, since Judith didn't walk, a short cut was taken. When she was in a drugged stupor, she signed a paper approving the surgery. The shortcut procedure was simpler. They simply cut off the tops of both femurs - the tops of the bones of her legs. They used that bone for the fusion in her back. Her legs were left dangling. The hip cavity in her pelvis was left empty. I was in shock. It explained why

Judith's legs were so short. Gradually, the shortened bones had withdrawn back into the pelvis.

On the appointed day in March, 1988, Judith and I went to Mount Sinai Hospital, orthopaedic wing for our examination. In due course, after everyone else was done, we were given a cubicle. I got Judith on the examining gurney we had acquired. This was not a small accomplishment since friends are not allowed in. Waving 4" of x-rays and looking both determined and confident, I became the brother who refused to be budged. The first mini crisis was in the x-ray room. They wouldn't let me stay. I relaxed my vigilance for a moment. Because they were not used to handling Judith, particularly under these circumstances, they pushed and pulled to get x-rays and generated new and original pain.

Later, a pleasant resident asked me (not Judith) what was wrong with her. Judith responded with a detailed lecture on orthopaedic surgical techniques which the resident admitted was beyond her. She had not done that part of the residency yet.

Finally we got to see the orthopaedic surgeon. He studied the old x-rays, then the new ones in total disbelief. His face betrayed his disgust at the experimental procedure. His only comment, "This procedure has been abolished for years." His tone was not complimentary.

He interpreted the plates. Simply, the old jagged femur ends which had been left dangling had progressively grown (calcified) back into her pelvis. From the surgeon's angry mumbling, we learned that calcification could not have occurred unless the capping was done badly. Judith had known this for years, but now it was "explained". Thus, every movement of Judith legs/hips broke the fusion. There was jagged bone everywhere inside the pelvis. Infection was rampant. On the spot, he grounded Judith. She was not even to get back into her wheelchair. He was explicit. The slightest wrong move could slice nerves or arteries.

This was a new problem. Judith wanted to continue life. The obvious solution was a hospital gurney which would allow her to keep her hips steady and still get about town. The hospital could/would not release one. Further enquiries got the same answer. Never to be thwarted by "can't", Judith called her friend, John McKnight in Chicago. In Chicago you can get anything for money. We acquired a gurney in three days. Typically, Judith moved her bed into the back of her van, drove to Chicago and collected the gurney on the weekend. So much for "you can't get around."

Two additional issues were raised by the doctor. He would have to get the infection under control before surgery was possible. Secondly, since the surgery was elective, getting theatre time would be a problem. On the positive side, he said that the technical part of the surgery, scraping out the pelvic fusion and capping the femurs appropriately, was relatively straight forward. He noted that Judith would make history once again. You cannot have this operation twice - except for Judith.

Three months passed. The infection cleared. Judith's back strain had eased adequately to schedule surgery. Putting together a surgical team may seem to be an ordinary task, but nothing is ordinary for Judith. Given their training, most medical practitioners cannot understand how or why Judith is alive - or even worse - why she would want to live. Thus, selecting a surgical team was another hurdle.

Finally, a team was assembled. Judith was admitted to Toronto General. The Joshua Committee met with Judith's attendants. We agreed that she could not be alone in the hospital. It was too dangerous. We simply transferred their "work station" to the hospital. It took some time for the nurses to get used to the idea of Judith's attendants "living in". They soon learned that it eased their work load. The attendants could take care of Judith better than they could. The attendants were more experienced. The wait began.

They Meant No Harm - But...

The first appointed surgery day arrived, Friday June 3. At the last minute, an anaesthesiologist (part of the team) who had neglected to see Judith until midnight (surgery scheduled in a.m.) cancelled the surgery. He ordered four months of tests to be completed before he would allow the team to proceed. We raised hell, called in all our "doctor chits", and had all the tests done in a day.

We were ready to proceed, but needed a new anaesthesiologist. It was a surprise, but we were ready to go again Sunday morning. Judith had explained that a tracheostomy (cutting a breathing hole in the wind pipe) would likely be a good idea. But she was only a lay person. What could she possibly know? Judith was taken into "pre-op" and the team administered the anaesthetic.

None of us were allowed in the prep room. If we had fought harder, maybe we could have avoided the near tragedy that followed. Typically, the theatre was so booked that even though Judith was a special case, no one had really checked her over very carefully in advance. After one doctor administered the pre-anaesthetic, they took the standard adult intubator (breathing) tube and began to stuff it down Judith's throat. It wouldn't fit. They lubricated it and pushed harder.

Although Judith was conscious, she couldn't signal her agony. They shoved harder. She began to suffocate and her heart stopped. Then they freaked out. Judith survived, but, they literally shredded the interior of her throat. They admitted they had nearly lost her. It had been too close for comfort.

IF anyone had explained what was going to happen, this could have been avoided. If they had asked Judith, or any of us, we would have told them that since she had never walked or run, her throat was underdeveloped - and child size. All they had to do was use a smaller intubator tube. No one thought of that. No one asked. A modern medical team nearly killed her. Needless to say, the operation was cancelled again. Now Judith had to recover from the anaesthetic poisoning. More time.

The following morning, after Judith and I left emergency recovery, we were informed that "no anaesthesiologist would touch Judith". By implication, she could just stay on her back forever. Judith was not enthralled by the idea, but was planning life regardless. The personal trauma she endured without vocalizing a word must have been horrendous. She had just spent three months on her back. She had managed to continue to function full steam ahead - wheelchair or no wheelchair. She had quietly concluded that any place she could get in a wheelchair, she could get in a gurney. We got her a new computer which she could operate totally with a mouth straw. By the time she arrived in the hospital, she was typing papers at 35 words per minute - with her mouth. But after three months of gurney experience, she was determined to proceed - somehow.

Another two weeks passed. The infection and anaesthetic were finally under control. But then nerves started to fray. There was still no surgery date. Our deadlines were fast approaching. The McGill Summer Institute opened at the beginning of July. Judith & Marsha taught a course together. Even more important, Judith was getting married (that will come next) on July 23. She was determined to be sitting up in her wheelchair for her wedding. If the surgery wasn't booked soon, she was determined to take her chances till after the wedding.

If we had been concerned about the potential of the medical system to hurt Judith before, we now moved to red alert. In addition to medical issues, there was stress. The first layer was simply being in hospital. Most human beings don't choose it as a place of residence willingly. For Judith it was torture. And now, everyone was tense. The wedding date in July was looming, and we all knew that if they didn't move quickly, it would be a repeat of the whole procedure later. And there was a new issue. We put out our sensors to find out what had happened and what was next on the medical front. While it had been difficult assembling a surgery team for this botched attempt, we were worried that now Judith would be black listed. We were right. No anaesthesiologist would touch her after that last episode. Regardless of who was right or wrong, there was the matter of insurance rates to consider. Then we heard on the grape vine that another member of the surgical team had said, "What does it matter if she sits up. What does she have to live for anyway?" The implication was that she should stay bed ridden for life. But the medical staff view of Judith was not of a person. She was just another messy case, better ignored. So they ignored her.

That was when we rallied the troops again. We got our doctor and friend, Yves Talbot, the head of Family Practice at Mount Sinai to intervene. Yves was a good friend and had been gently pressuring behind the scenes earlier. Now he made a few calls.

A new surgical team had to be assembled. From the start, there was a condition - use a tracheostomy for breathing. Judith wasn't excited, but she was fully aware that a trach was always probable for her - if anyone had asked. She agreed. We found an anaesthesiologist who was willing. A surgical team was assembled. Then we began to lobby for theatre time. Judith had been waiting, complete with an I-V tube in her neck for two weeks. We were all going stir-crazy. The first of many dates was set. There were always last minute cancellations. More waiting. One side benefit was that Judith grew stronger after the anaesthetic poisoning. She also grew more anxious - and crotchety. Who wouldn't?

Meanwhile, Laurence, the groom in waiting, called from Alberta regularly, but much to our collective but unstated surprise, he remained in Alberta.

We only had 24 hours notice with a firm surgery booking. This was delayed for another 24 hours. Then, they took Judith!

Finally Judith had the surgery. It was such a relief. She survived and discovered almost immediately what it was like to live without constant pain. She had some new unexpected agony. The prognosis was complex. The orthopaedic surgery had gone well. The femurs were capped, the pelvic cavity scraped clean and smooth. Her hips (with no hip bones) should now be able to move easily and painlessly. But there were new leg pains. At first no one listened. Then, under protest, after four days, and this time with an attendant, Judith went for x-rays. A broken leg. Under the anaesthetic, she was unable to scream when people pushed and pulled her body. It was and is more fragile than many. Once again, one would have hoped (vainly) that the team might have been extra careful. But after all that, it was a minor problem. All in all it worked. And if the healing went quickly, Judith would be sitting for her wedding.

Judith was relieved once she found out that she had only a broken leg. We proceeded with her schedule to get her talking. Then there was the tracheostomy. The medical team wanted to leave her hooked up for a week. We of course plugged up the little hole in Judith's throat almost immediately. This allowed Judith to talk, and ensured that her body wouldn't relax and get used to not breathing adequately to allow her to speak. In tiny gasps, Judith practised breathing and speaking. The first few words were faint, but they were welcome to all of us. Gradually, we would cover the hole and let her talk for a few words at a time. We were all on the mend. After about 5 days, we blocked the hole and decided to move out of the hospital. We didn't want to risk any more Iatrogenic diseases! (Iatrogenic refers to new diseases/injuries and illnesses that patients acquire in hospitals in addition and unrelated to their initial problem - as a result of medical "treatment".)

We had Judith out of the hospital in record time. We found out much later how much ahead of schedule we were. A doctor friend ran into one of the supervising medical staff and enquired about Judith. "Oh yeah, the quad on the 4th floor. I haven't seen her for a bit, but it will be 3-4 months before I'll sign her release papers." Our friend said nothing. He knew that she had already been in Montreal, teaching at the McGill Summer Institute with Marsha, and he had been a guest at Judith's wedding. She had rolled out of the hospital and gone to McGill on her own gurney. She was in her chair for her wedding. She spent the summer travelling, teaching and carrying on business as usual. After all, what would you expect of a new bride.

The Big C's - California And Cancer...

In the middle of this, having just moved Marsha's mother (who was also very ill) to Toronto, and having survived several job related crises, Marsha and I decided we needed to see a little daylight. On May 13, we ran to California for 10 days to walk and talk and recover. We climbed every small mountain on Big Sur. It was glorious. We needed it. It was a beginning - with fortuitous timing. We arrived back to discover that Marsha's regular medical (including a routine mammogram) turned up cancer signals. We both were traumatized. Marsha was booked into Mount Sinai Hospital for exploratory surgery, across the street from the Toronto General Hospital where Judith was hospitalized. We got the news on a Friday, June 10, had the surgery on Monday morning, June 13, and left for Colorado on Thursday afternoon. Marsha was the keynote speaker for the State Convention of the ARC (Association for Retarded Citizens).   We got the call from the surgeon Friday morning, June 14, 20 minutes before Marsha's talk. Introductory malignant cancer of the breast. The surgeon took the five minutes he had to try and explain that the surgery he had done (a lumpectomy) was likely to be a complete cure, but those words sound very hollow after "cancer". Marsha gave a brilliant keynote. I was numb. When we returned we did more tests. And now there are checkups. So far so good.

I was beside myself. The stress around Judith was substantial - after months of hospitals and run arounds. Both Marsha and Judith in hospital at the same time was a bit beyond my capacity to endure. I have very limited recall of those critical days. The memory does wonderful things in wiping out pain.

There is a median between the two hospitals on University Avenue. I felt like I was living there - on the median. I also remember that Judith had some "Rescue Remedy" - a tiny bottle. She instructed me that immediately after surgery, I was to put four drops under her tongue - and to do the same for Marsha. I remember standing in the median with a tiny bottle of rescue remedy - praying that whatever it was - those drops would revive both Judith and Marsha to full health - miraculously. I was ready for a miracle.

As fate would have it, the operations were virtually simultaneous. Judith's first (attempted) surgery was followed by Marsha, then the confirmation of malignancy, then Judith's second and successful attempt. It is just a terrible blur. I do remember giving Judith her drops - and then racing to give Marsha hers, and then Judith again. I don't remember if I took any.

Marsha was amazing. She came out of the anaesthetic in record time. She was determined not to hang around the hospital for one second more than necessary. Later, she described her deep breathing exercises as she came out of the anaesthetic. By the time I gave her the drops, she was bright as a pin. She got dressed and we left. It was a bit of a shock to the hospital staff. Patients in North America don't get up and walk away from the hospital two hours after surgery. Marsha did. We walked across the street to visit Judith.

Judith came around more slowly. They had finally operated. She had been nearly 4 hours "under the knife". She was also verbally disabled - since the tracheostomy prevented her from talking. But in her own inimitable style, Judith had planned ahead. She had worked out a "thumb code" using Morse Code. Thus, she was unable to talk - but fully able to communicate. The surgeon was dumb struck. I was overwhelmed with relief as Marsha was alive and Judith was communicating - both having survived surgical traumas.

Marsha's post surgical review was excellent. The malignant spots were very early and tiny. Dr. Irv Koven, our excellent surgeon, was very confident that he had got all the mutant cells. He gave us an A+ rating for the future. I say us, because, I felt like we had the cancer together, and together we will heal and regain our balance.

The Wedding

The Wedding....Judith and Laurence's

With the benefit of 20-20 hindsight, everyone now says, "They shouldn't have got married!" True, Judith and Laurence are separated and they have discussed divorce - just like half of all modern marriages in Canada. But I don't see why that turns into, "they shouldn't have married." Judith and Laurence are adults, over 21 and consenting. They knew the risks. They also deluded each other equally into believing that "the other person" would change. None of this is original. It happens with almost every new couple. They have the right to make responsible mistakes - just like the rest of us. Fortunately for them, I think they were both quick to realize that it wasn't working. The greater risk was to stay together and destroy each other. So they are separated and may get divorced. It has been painful for both, but that is part of life in the 90's. They have learned and are breaking up in a humane manner.

As we review galleys for the press, the next phase of this marriage saga is emerging. The discussions of divorce have been put on hold. Judith has put her wedding ring back on. In long distance calls and letters, Judith and Laurence have rediscovered some of the magic that brought them together initially. They have discovered that they are still committed to each other. Ironically, like the rest of us, they assumed that the answer to their relationship was a traditional marriage. Perhaps once again, Judith will be a pioneer. They may well invent a new model of long distance relationship that is healthy and nurturing and supportive and loving. We'll all have to wait and see what life brings. This isn't an issue about handicap. It is about how we choose to live our lives. It is the same for all of us.

The tale I want to tell does not focus on the breakup. We all know those stories too well. Rather, I want to talk about the romance - and the wedding. It was a great celebration. Divorce or not, it was worth it - at least for me.

My version of this romance is mine. I don't claim it has any accuracy other than being my perspective. Judith has always been a person who wanted to push the limits - to experience everything. She is a terror on wheels, and has done more, travelled further, explored deeper than most other human beings I have known. The limitations of her physical being were very inconvenient, but not a barrier. Thus, as Judith reached 35, like many unmarried men and women, she began to stir. "If I don't get married soon, I won't marry at all". When Judith began to talk about marriage, those of us who knew her assumed it was virtually a 'fait accompli'. There were some missing details - like a groom. But once Judith had made up her mind, it was time to plan the guest list.

Not everyone was so enthusiastic. In fact, almost no one.

People kept asking "why?" I don't think anyone had the courage to say what they were thinking out loud. Judith talking about marriage was like one of those little "black flies" that brings buried anger and confusion to the fore. Under their breath, people muttered, "She can't have sex anyway... Why would she bother to get married?... She can't have a baby... She should be thankful with what she's got... She should be realistic! ... Who would marry her anyway?" I never heard any of these questions because both Marsha and I always took the precaution of announcing our unqualified enthusiasm for the wedding before anyone stepped in the cow-pie. But I saw the questions in people's eyes and we heard gossip. It is also interesting how we all jump to conclusions. There is absolutely no reason that Judith cannot enjoy a sexual relationship. We often leap to unwarranted and invalid conclusions when we don't check the facts.

Then there was another element. Jealousy. For some women, Judith had always aroused antagonism because she was supposedly not physically beautiful. Yet the power of her mind and spirit was enormously attractive to people - including many men. Thus, if Judith could marry, some felt that it relegated them to second best. "They" couldn't compete with Judith because she was brilliant, and she could use her handicap to manipulate people. It seems ironic, but Judith threatened many women. The antagonism was revealed in strange ways. The discussion of her intent to marry was one.

For men, the issue of Judith marrying was different. I suppose it really focused us on the issue of the nature of marriage. What is it really about? Is it about sex? And what kind of sex? How important is it? Or is marriage more about love, respect, relationship - being together. Judith's exploration of marriage and sexuality challenged many to consider their own values - and to genuinely think about the meaning of marriage - of being intimate partners for life. There was also likely an element of pity in the thinking of many men. Marrying Judith was an opportunity to demonstrate personal "martyrdom" - to give yourself to a life of sacrifice. I say this not with any sense of condemnation. Anyone raised in the Christian tradition would likely have explored the mental gymnastics of self sacrifice as a gesture of Christian charity. I think it is illusory and wrong, but I am sure it played a role.

And then there was Judith. She wanted to experience life. Marriage was part of life. Why should she be denied the dignity of risk.

I could think up dozens of logical argument. We reviewed them at Joshua Committee meetings, not as moral directives, but as issues we would have to deal with if Judith married. For example, the attendant care system, which was for the first time in recent years functioning with just normal personnel crises, could be exploded.

Externally, the government might interpret a husband as having legal and moral obligations to both pay for attendant care, and also to be an attendant. Judith's position was very simple. A husband is a husband. An attendant is an attendant. They can meet over tea - but they are distinct. Her position was clear - but when setting precedents in social policy, nothing is clear or obvious. I raised the issue that we must be prepared to battle for this independence should it arise.

I had been hoping that no one would bring up the topic of marriage at any of our funding meetings. I specifically cautioned Judith to be silent. But her boundless enthusiasm triumphed. We were meeting with our new COMSOC officer. To my eternal horror, Judith bubbled over about her impending marriage. Once again we were blessed with a supportive official. He mumbled, "I didn't hear that - right?" I assured him his hearing was picking up external distortions.

Internally, we were also concerned. An attendant care system designed to flow with the needs and desires of one person - especially a Judith Snow - is enormously complex. Adding a husband into the social dynamics of "attendant care" could well be explosive - and thus dangerous to Judith. We were concerned about issues like personality clashes, jealousy, territorial rights, and personal styles. As it turned out, these were in fact real issues. Two tiny examples make the point. Laurence placed the tooth paste one place, the attendants another. This was a serious irritant. Judith insisted it must be in place "A". Her reasoning was that she could not get in the bathroom, thus had to be able to tell attendants where it was. It must be in the same place at all times. Laurence, also an adult of fixed patterns (and who isn't), felt that the toothpaste should/could be moved. It wasn't a big accommodation. But there were two strong willed adults, bachelors used to living on their own - in their own way. Clearly toothpaste wasn't the issue. But I can assure you that enormous energy was committed to sorting the placement of the Crest - to avoid tremors that might have registered 7.5 on the Richter scale.

Tea was also an issue. It nearly tore apart the attendant care system. Laurence liked tea. Reasonable. He felt that if Judith asked the attendants to make him a cup of tea, they should. They were "her hands". They would do it for any of Judith's other guests - as part of their job. But they argued. Laurence wasn't just any other guest. They would make tea for Judith. But, they weren't there to be servants for Laurence... Interesting and explosive. We nearly lost it. Tea and toothpaste. They weren't the issues, but that is how the tension was played out. Just like all the rest of us.

Marsha and others spent substantial blocks of time on special attendant care briefing meetings. We tried all the usual accommodations. They didn't work.

I haven't forgotten the wedding. I'm just working back to it, and now up to it.

The Romance...

Judith had many male friends. When she decided she wanted to get married, it was a matter of doing a scan, and exploring some options. Laurence Hunt was a charming, handsome, gentle, intelligent friend. He was a psychologist by training, but in Judith's life he was one of the volunteer (unpaid) attendants who had become a friend. He was deeply religious and they enjoyed exploring that mutual commitment. Laurence was also extremely organized - some would say fastidious. However, in managing an attendant care system, commitment to detail is a matter of life and death. Thus, as Laurence moved into the foreground of romance, Judith began to fantasize about not having to worry about her attendant care system - even just for a few hours a day. Laurence might be able to do it. That may seem like a strange fantasy, but for a person who has never been able to relax, even for a moment, being able to rely on someone absolutely was indeed a fantasy.

One of the quirks of history is that Laurence was offered a very good job in northern Alberta. Since he needed income, he went. Thus, the romance, like many others, was largely by telephone and letters. And perhaps that is how the fantasy grew unchecked. But it did, and both willing partners loved it - as we all do. It was a Harlequin romance. What could be better for Judith and Laurence?

There was alternative writing on the wall. I read it at the time, but there are some billboards that are better ignored. We ignored the signs. There were too many other issues to deal with. Firstly, Judith's family. They were not impressed. And don't fall into the trap that "they should have been different." Judith's parents were just plain solid citizens. They didn't have degrees in handicapism. They had to learn the real way - from their daughter. Thus, as human beings, every new challenge was new and stirred up the full range of emotion and turmoil. But, once it was clear that Judith had decided, the family changed gears. We all moved into wedding mode.

For many years, there had been tension between Judith and her family - her mother in particular. Judith often told the story that in her family there were three children and "the project". She was the "project". No one intended that, but such sentiments are imbedded very deeply in the soul. Although the family had done what few could do, there was tension - which is also normal.

The Wedding Planning Committee...

As much as Judith was looking forward to the wedding, she was dreading the planning. That's where we all came in. And from my perspective, it was fascinating and wonderful. We established the wedding planning committee. It was a sub-committee of the Joshua Committee with a whole new spectrum of helpers. Many of the women from Judith's Church were members. Meetings were scheduled in Judith's apartment. I was officially the minute taker - and unofficially the referee. At some of the meetings, I called the game early - when the ice started to melt.

The physical layout of these encounters of the fourth kind said everything. If it were an ice hockey rink, Judith parked herself (riding high on her gurney) in front of the goal at one end of the room, and her mother, protected the opposing net. The rest of us formed a gauntlet as remarks were traded up and down the line. The topics were "how many guests, decorations, banquet menu, location, dress, bridesmaids, and other wedding stuff". The real content was even more fascinating. I don't think either Judith or her mother realized what was happening for quite a while. By then, they both treasured it too dearly to mention it. What was really happened was that Judith's mother decided that "when my daughters get married, they will do it right!" She might also have added "my way". But Mrs. Rita Snow geared up to "marry her daughter". It was something she was familiar with. She had strong opinions and she made them very clear. There was no question regarding where Judith got her determination.

Judith was equally strong willed. She wanted (as do most daughters) to have "her" wedding - and not have the whole thing planned by and for her mother. There was a clash of wills - and details. I ran interference. Rita Snow wanted it "proper". Judith, midway through her hippie period, (twenty years behind the times, and decades ahead of society), was shall we say, less interested in convention.

In the process, a miracle occurred. Judith suddenly realized that for the first time in years, perhaps in her life, her mother was fighting for and with her - as a daughter. She wasn't "the project". She was a daughter of the Snow family. And daughters of the Snow family get married "correctly".

Rita saw it too. She saw, perhaps for the first time, not a 38 year old project in a wheelchair, but a young woman in love - her daughter getting married. Their battles were the battles of every mother-daughter in wedding planning. There was no "disability" issue on the table. There was no "able" and no "disabled". It was a struggle between a mother and a daughter that was typical, generational and beautiful. The issue was a planning for a wedding. And what a wedding it was.

The Wedding...

Needless to say, we had a rehearsal, and a dinner, and a reception at Frontier College the night before. We did it all.

The wedding was July 23, 1988 at Eglinton United Church in Toronto. It was a remarkable celebration of life. For Judith, Marsha and I, it had special significance since we had all just survived major trials. It transcended all our immediate crises and was a statement about how life could be lived in an alternative future. Judith does have a very complex physical disability, but this wedding had nothing to do with disability. It had to do with living life to the limits.

Over two hundred friends and relatives arrived - from all over United States and Canada, and from England. Rita hand made gorgeous ribboned bouquets that adorned the front pews in the Church. As people streamed in, there was an atmosphere of ecstasy - enchantment. It was likely living a fairy tale. There were dozens and dozens of families whose young children would never have to fight some battles because of Judith's pioneering life. And they were there to share in their friend's jubilation. Greg Hoskins and his band had composed a song. Once all the computer synthesizers were powered up, they filled the church with the mixed sweet sounds of voices, sax, keyboard and guitar.

We had installed a ramp onto the stage, so when the bridal party emerged, they "arose". Judith's father, Ted, beamed as he watched his daughter enter the Sanctuary, while he hosted the British family visitors. Judith was positively resplendent. It was amazing. I don't think anyone really saw a wheelchair that day. The glow on Judith's face so captivated one's attention that our perceptions were altered - at least for the day, and for some, forever.

Two ministers officiated, Orville Endicott and Sylvia Hamilton. In front of a beautiful symbolic tapestry, stitched by Rita's loving fingers, each minister put on one ring. It was beautiful. Marsha was Matron of Honour. Marie McLean, (Judith's favourite attendant now visiting from her home in Nova Scotia) and Judith's sister were the bride's maids. They positively effervesced. Judith's nephew's carried banners high, proud and crimson. Another niece and nephew - flower girl and ring bearer. Midway through the service, Laurence and Judith invited the children to the pulpit to talk about what this wedding meant to them.

At the penultimate moment, as the new bride and groom turned to greet the multitude, Judith and Laurence invited everyone to participate in "agape" - the symbolic breaking of bread together in celebration. We distributed bread and grapes. All of us in the bridal party "went forth" and while Greg played, shared the triumphant ecstasy of friends gathered in the sanctuary for this celebration of life. It was a sight to share and behold.

It was one of Judith's ideas. It was wonderful. It allowed everyone to radiate their emotion - some with tears, some with cheers. There was a communal outpouring of emotion that was appropriate to the occasion.

I took photographs. It was easy. Judith and Laurence were a "picture" of joy and rapture. Later, after pictures on the lawn, and more pictures, and more pictures, we all filed into the Church hall for a buffet banquet. It took me a little longer since the lawn was damp, and being in an exceptionally frivolous mood, Judith "stood" on my shoe. I ended up taking all the pictures - on a damp lawn - in stocking feet.

The reception in the evening was a continuation of that same spirit of triumph. The lines were long. People were talking. It was a social event in every sense. Friends from across the city and continent were renewed by the opportunity - and by the crackling energy of the occasion. I acted as Master of Ceremonies. The presentations to the newlyweds were extensive. Poems were read, songs written, gifts presented. John McKnight and Barbara Morford, friends from Chicago, read and presented a beautiful scroll - and carved weather vanes - for free spirits. Rebecca Lusthaus composed and sang her own song. The list of speakers was like a "who's who" of North American integration. Perhaps the most telling comment was by Bob Williams, the Washington lobbyist who spelled out his message on his communication board. Bob Perske, the noted author from Connecticut, and the friend in the "Bob and Bob Duo", spoke Williams' quips to us. "Governor Dukakis has just borrowed a new word in his campaign for the American Presidency - the word community. He should be here to understand what it means."

It was an event. But perhaps the most profound happening was missed by most. Judith thanked her parents, and they in turn blessed their daughter at her wedding. That's what love and marriage - and family is about. Judith's wedding had it in abundance.

I don't recall a wedding quite like it. I had never been on a wedding planning committee before so perhaps I had missed something. But somehow, I think this was very special. At least it was for me.

And now, as too often happens, Judith and Laurence have grown apart. They will be friends again - soon - because they are both fine people. They will struggle through the darkness of separation and find new resolution. But I choose to think that no matter what, no one - especially Judith and Laurence - will ever regret one of the great weddings and celebrations of my life time.

Circle Activities
Institutions &
Attendant Care

Then the Perske's Wrote "Circles of Friends"...

I am definitely a slow learner in some areas. I had been living the reality of the Joshua Committee for years. We had weathered one crisis after another. We were very close friends. But still I didn't see anything extraordinary. It just seemed like common sense. It wasn't as if I didn't know differently. In just about every community I encountered through Frontier College, I saw people struggling in isolation, alone, unsupported. I saw a society with virtually no stable relationships - and few friends. I had no excuses for my oversight.

When Bob Perske, the American author who writes about friendship, came and spent time with us in the fall of 1987, he interviewed us all at length. I had a feeling he must be seeing something. He took photos, and his artist-partner and wife, Martha, drew a portrait of the Joshua Committee. It was stunning. I guess that was when I realized out loud that what we had been doing was something very special and unusual. I think now that my unconscious oversight was a way of avoiding the pain - the painful awareness of how impossible life must be for so many lonely people.

The Perske's book, <u>Circles of Friends</u>, was published in 1988. It was a runaway best seller in its category. Bob was asked to do the keynote address at the national TASH Conference (The Association for the Severely Handicapped) in Chicago that year. He read his story of the Joshua Committee. That was when I finally realized that our lives were not "normal", that the Joshua Committee was not regular, and that Judith was not just another friend. Both Marsha and Judith had known it for years. I denied the obvious for good reasons. I believed then and still do today that anyone and everyone should have friends; that a Joshua Committee can be for anyone; and that it is entirely possible. I wanted to see it as so simple, that I denied its pioneering role and example. No more. I see it for what it is. But I still believe that it is very common sense stuff, and that anyone who wants a friend can do it.

Bradwin Speaker - Oct. 22, 1988

The Frontier College Annual Meeting has a fine tradition. Honouring the name of Bradwin, the second Principal, each year an eminent Canadian who has an important message of relevance to the College is asked to speak. Judith was that eminent Canadian in 1988 - the 89th Annual Meeting of the College. Her very presence was a precedent, but Judith lived up to the tradition. Judith also knew it was an opportunity to do something for me. Her speech was enormously affirming at a time when I needed it.

Judith spoke about her experience of living on the margins of society - and her battle to be a participating citizen. She spoke about her vision of a community with the capacity to include ALL People in all their diversity. She quoted from Isaiah to remind us that if we do not welcome the gifts of the stranger, we are doomed to slowly crumble under our own inertia. She reminded us that ordinary people have the gift of everydayness, but if we are to cope with the challenge of change, we need to identify those with the gifts of surviving and growing through change. "This is the gift of the outcast... Living on the margin either burns you out and kills you, or it turns you into a dreamer, someone who really knows what sort of change will help and who can just about taste it; someone who is prepared to do anything to bring about change. If these dreamers are liberated, if they are brought back into the arms of society, they become the architects of the new community; a community that has a new capacity to support everyone's needs and interactions." Judith challenged all of us to ally ourselves with dreamers on the edge.

Judith could not be seen following the speech. Everyone was standing - an ovation. But the glow emanating from the front of the room assured one and all that their resident visionary was very present. [Judith's Bradwin address is appendix 1-A]

Judith Sleeps With Bradley...

This was going on before Judith was married. They still snuggle every night. But the truth is that Bradley is Judith's breathing machine. She wears it at night to keep the air pressure up in her lungs when she is sleeping. Bradley was the name of the doctor who solved the problem. Judith does love and honour some doctors.

Judith was about 36 and actually doing really well. That is when she began to have new breathing problems. At first it was just being tired, and that took its toll. But it grew worse. She couldn't sleep at night - because when she actually dropped off, she stopped breathing. She would awake - gasping for air - and increasingly more terrified of going to sleep and not being able to wake herself in time to restore her breathing. Needless to say this gradually infringed on her general health as well.

We began another round of doctors. Because Judith was always napping for a few seconds here and there, we checked out narcolepsy. It didn't really wash. Neither did anything else. Then a creative open minded doctor called Bradley began thinking about the fact that Judith didn't breath very deeply - sitting in a wheelchair and with no limb movements. He had a very simple thought - oxygen deprivation. He hypothesized that limited movement meant limited oxygen flow. Further, at night, when Judith wasn't consciously deep breathing and talking, the chest muscles relaxed and the oxygen flow decreased further. As the brain oxygen decreased, so did the responsiveness of the abdominal breathing muscles - thus the cycle of deprivation grew worse until Judith either choked - or went into a coma. He didn't think that Judith's chest muscles were going to respond to exercises - so he wondered about simply increasing the oxygen flow - reversing the air pressure - to keep her lungs full of air at night. "Bradley" was invented. He is a small air pump hooked to a small face mask. Judith wears the Bradley mask in bed. The pump is very gentle. It doesn't interfere with breathing out. But when Judith breathes in, it supplements the "inflow" that stronger muscles would draw in naturally - thus increasing the oxygen in her lungs.

Judith's zest for life literally changed over night. Within a week of sleeping with Bradley, her colour was back and she was in fighting trim. It's nice to have someone like Bradley to sleep with.

Vive la Difference...

This is the fifth year. Amazing. Time flies. It began one night at Yves Talbot's house. Yves, head of Family Practice at Mount Sinai Hospital, was concerned about what students did not know about "Life" as they left with their MD's under their stethoscopes. He asked Marsha and I if we would help invent a course to introduce the students to other realities.

We left in the wee hours of the morning. We had titled the course "Vive la Difference" and planned ten weekly seminars introducing students to new realities. We planned to advertise the course by announcing that students would have to choose it as their first elective, and that a pre-condition was that they would have to "be willing to change their lives". I think Yves was the one in deepest shock. I know now that he was both suspect and frightened by what he had unleashed.

To our collective shock, students applied. We began with a dozen - our self imposed limit. Our agenda was to introduce the students to "real people" who came from very different realities, but with whom they would likely interact as physicians. We wanted them to understand that not everyone thinks, speaks, acts, and reacts the same. We wanted them to appreciate their own biases - as biases - but to surmount them to treat patients as people. We wanted to teach them to listen.

Our methodology was simple. Judith was and still is a key part of it. We tried to meet on "local turf" of various interest groups, rather than in a medical classroom. In Judith's case, we gathered in her apartment. It was crowded but wonderful. We positioned everyone so they had to assist Judith, and give her tea. Judith was a very willing participant since we all knew that these young impressionable people would be doctors. They would have the power of life and death over people like Judith. They could set the tone for a life of possibilities - or a life of misery. We saw it as an important inroad.

The sessions with Judith were always profound. She told her own story. Often the students got defensive. "Doctors" wouldn't do that... That is when Yves would chime in. "Yes they do. What Judith is telling you happens every day. Just yesterday in emergency..." But Judith also set the tone for the course. She talked about deinstitutionalization and life - and living in the community. She talked about having friends. She laid the ground work for dignity and morality as criteria - rather than simply economics and scheduling. We learned more each year that as important as the words were, it was the experience that hit people. Being in Judith's apartment; feeding her a muffin; trying to understand how the best medical system in Canada could have put her on a geriatric ward. It didn't make sense. But it did of course - from one perspective.

And so as the classes encountered real people that lived in realities beyond their experience and imagination. The course gradually challenged the fundamental values of much of medicine. It dealt with simple truths like having a home, having friends, living and being a participant in a community. We think it created a climate to foster a new kind of doctor.

Judith began as one of the presenters. Now she is part of our little faculty. This past year, when Marsha and I were in Asia, Judith and Yves taught the course together. They both learned a great deal. Judith learned about her almost uncontrolable distrust of doctors - which she has under control because of Yves. Yves learned that Judith is a person - not just an interesting patient. Funny how things happen. Although the course still has no budget, it is up for awards for excellence. And although none of us have had time to write about it, three medical schools have asked us to assist them in developing a similar model. Clearly we have touched a nerve in modern medicine. And once again, Judith was a visionary in leading the way.

Eternal Vigilance - the Price of Freedom & Survival

This year, while I was away on sabbatical after 15 years as the President of Frontier College, Judith was attacked. We had made the College into a safe harbour for over a decade, but on April 30, 1990, Judith was informed that the Executive Committee of the Board had passed a resolution stating that the College wanted to phase out of handling her contracts immediately. The first contract, her salary and expenses from Secretary of State was moveable, and that was done forthwith. Due to the strong support for Judith from individuals in government, the transfer to another sponsor was permitted without incident. However, the attendant care contract was also to be "dumped". I worked on that contract for 11 years, and shared the scars with Judith for making the precedents. I knew that transferring the contract was perhaps impossible, and at best, a risky and complex bureaucratic process. Thus, simply to announce that the College would not renew her contract was to virtually ensure the collapse of 11 years of precedent setting work and condemn Judith to death on a geriatric ward - the only creative alternative government agencies had been able to devise for her.

I was very upset when the College attacked Judith. She has been one of my greatest teachers. Everyone was quite emotional the evening of May 2nd, when we regrouped the Joshua Committee to defend Judith's life. For any normal person, it is a shock to be told to pick up your contracts and get out. For Judith, it was a death threat. In my initial reaction, I questioned whether this was actually an attack on me, via Judith. It is fascinating to speculate on plots and schemes, but the reality was likely more prosaic - and therefore, ultimately more deadly. Most people could not and did not appreciate the delicate structure of Judith's funding spider web. They should have, but they never asked me or Judith, and they likely didn't know. They just acted. Judith was being discarded for obscure unstated reasons of bureaucratic convenience. She was messy and hard to make neat and tidy.

This is precisely the history of human services. No one meant to do harm. However, ignorance and lack of careful attention once again put Judith's life on the line. It was another terrifying symbol of how institutions and systems, no matter how caring, can hurt people. Careful investigation would have revealed a structure so intricate that one would only tinker with great care. Then again, why tinker at all? Judith was once again put at risk.

I had just arrived back from five months in Asia on the Friday evening (April 27). Judith was informed of the decision of the Executive Committee of Frontier College on Monday (April 30). The Joshua Committee convened a formal emergency meeting Wednesday evening (May 2). The following day there was a formal request for a meeting with the College and a strong letter presented. We decided I should not be present. My presence might complicate the central issue which was the maintenance of Judith's contracts - her survival. Meanwhile, we contacted officials at Secretary of State in Ottawa. They quickly agreed to transfer Judith's employment contract to the Centre for Integrated Education and Community.

I had anticipated a relaxed reentry into Toronto in preparation for my return to Frontier College. However, none of that was to be. That week was Marsha's annual cancer check-up following surgery to excise a malignant cancer two years earlier. We were tense with anticipation. Once again, Marsha passed with flying colours, but we didn't know that on Monday.

On Thursday morning, (May 3) after trading messages, I had a brief unpleasant call. My Board Chair informed me that I was no longer welcome at Frontier College. After fifteen years of service, I was stunned! Given this background, it is comprehensible that I questioned whether the decision about Judith's contracts was part of a broader plan. To add to our paranoia, Marsha's contract with the College had been cut without consultation or discussion in March. A consulting report laced with misinformation and innuendo had proposed that the Centre for Integrated Education and

Community leave. Marsha moved the Centre immediately, but the atmosphere was icy and hardly filled with trust.

This is not about the College, so only the results of our intervention need be reported here. We won a reprieve. Judith's attendant care contract was extended. The Frontier College Board resolution at the end of May made it clear that the contract should move on, but only if and when it was secure. The Centre maintains an office in Frontier - Judith's office. It all worked out. The frustration is that none of the anguish endured to reach these very reasonable accommodations was necessary. The Centre was willing to move - but not to be shoved. I was ready to step down - but not to be dumped. Judith was flexible about contracts with the College - but not to the point of putting her survival at risk. None of these crises needed to be crises. But they were. And without vigilance, could have been disastrous. The College did not do its homework. Judith was put at risk, again.

It is always sobering when bureaucracy becomes the central value - rather than people - when the craving for neatness transcends vision. It can happen anywhere, anytime. Thus, in defending Judith, we were fighting for our dignity and our own survival. That is where it all began in 1979. This episode was just another example of the story of Judith's life - as I see it.

Attendant Care Action Coalition...
Just 10 Years of Work...

On May 31, 1990, Judith and colleagues gave a press conference at a major conference on Attendant Care. They announced that the Ministry of Community and Social Services would be announcing a new policy - a new program with "private" attendant care arrangements for up to 500 individuals in the first phase.

The timing of the Minister's announcement was a stunning coincidence. At 11:30 p.m. on the May 31, 1980, (a decade earlier to the day), officials of the Ministry had called requesting Frontier College to "handle" the first ever attendant care Order in Council contract. Ten years later - to the day, a policy we had dreamed of was announced. Funding would be available to individuals to allow them to live their own lives. Judith and I were both on the verge of new beginnings.

Twenty years of lobbying - with her life on the line - and finally a policy emerges. It was a good thing we chose to lobby for Judith in 1980 rather than waiting for the policy. Her headstone would long since have been covered with moss.

Part of the recent pressure for this policy began in 1986. Led by Judith, we were aware that things were "OK", but that complacency was settling in. The hard work on Orders in Council could be eroded in a minute. In fact, that spring, a directive nearly wiped out everyone on O.I.C. funding. That is when Judith rolled into action. She organized a meeting of nearly everyone affected. We held it at one of the attendant care supported apartment complexes down town. She had asked me to attend and facilitate with group graphics.

As usual, Judith had managed to get the key actors there -

both "consumers" and "providers". That night we formed the Attendant Care Action Coalition (ACAC). As is the case with most groups, it met irregularly and a few individuals did most of the work. But it kept meeting. And the reputation of ACAC exceeded it's size and capacity. They didn't let on. Letters from ACAC to the government, and from their Chair, Judith Snow, were listened to attentively.

Four years of meetings. I know that Judith had just about given up. She knew that a decision was being made and was terrified that once again they had come so close - and would be set aside for higher priorities. But on May 31, twenty years of hard work paid off. A new progressive policy is in place. It has the capacity for the first time to actually respond directly to people's needs.

I know that the next challenge of the Joshua Committee will be to make it work for Judith. After all, if it will work for Judith, it will work for anyone. Pioneering again - still - and I guess for ever more.

Judith - Colleague At Last..

"You turkey!" My remark to Judith certainly wasn't profound, but the issue was.

After all we had been through together, 11 years of struggle - including writing this book, I was stunned. In the fall of 1990, Judith finally admitted, "I think now I finally believe you and Marsha don't see me as a charity - a project - a cause. I know we are friends, but I was never sure that you really respected me as a colleague. Now I know."

I didn't know whether to be angry or simply incredulous. I couldn't believe that Judith thought that we thought... We laughed. It was the only reasonable response. I must admit it is a relief. However, since I didn't know it was an issue in the first place, it hasn't altered how we work together.

I have been dwelling on this. As I reflect, I recall one of the learnings - for which I require regular reminders. I learned that people who have lived on the margins have been wounded very deeply. I have learned that I - and I think most of us - grossly under estimate the severity of those scars. It takes an enormous commitment of time, support, love and respect to manage them. We cannot erase our past. We must learn to build on/over it. Many of us are adept at pretending "it never happened." This coping strategy is adequate for the short term, but not as a plan for life. Judith reminded me that even after 11 years of friendship, trust, working together, she still wasn't sure. That is the depth of the wounds. They never go away. There will always be doubts. All of us need support - life long. It isn't like a vaccination - once is not enough. So as Judith and Marsha and I begin our next decade of collaboration and friendship, I will remember the fragility of our security and the need for constant renewal.

I Was My Own Institution...

On November 11, 1990, we were in the kitchen - revising again. Producing a book turns out to be more work than we imagined. But as usual, Judith slips in those profound little comments as we sip tea.

We were talking about the "scars" - how deeply they cut. How slowly they heal. Judith tried to explain the unexplainable. I'll just let her talk:

"You know, until I was 30, I was my own institution - my

*own gate keeper. I bought into everything about institutional-
ization and admitted nothing - no information that did not fit.
I was not a person. I was an institution.*

*As I grew up, I lived a life like a puppet. There was no
Judith really. I was what I was supposed to be - and
simultaneously fighting what I was supposed to be. That is
why everything, every experience, kept turning back - fitting
back into the institutional mode.*

*It was only after I met Marsha that I began to get a
glimpse of the possibility of... It is really hard to say what it
is. I don't have words...the possibility of really being Judith.
That was the first time I/someone broke through my institutional wall and created the possibility of other possibilities.*

*I wear the "thunderbird" because it represents the essence
of who I am , a spiritual warrior. I never knew that I could
be that - I never even imagined - before I met Marsha.*

*For the first 3-5 years after we met, it was like shaking off
a sleep - a kind of unconsciousness - almost like shaking off a
chrysalis. I had to shake off a version of myself which never
was myself. Now it is different. It is more a matter of creating
the world within which I can be myself with my friends.
Together we are creating it. We really are creating it out of
nothing. We have to create the language, the vision, the
structures and the relationships. We create the meaning. All
that so we can be ourselves.*

*This explains the real differences of perception between
us. I would make a comment that would make you angry. I
would be puzzled why you were angry. But there is a massive
difference in perception. You see me as if I am changing
from a wounded to an unwounded person. For me, it is like I
am becoming a person instead of being nothing."*

Parenthood vs Attendant Care...

We had another profound conversation. Judith has had a difficult struggle communicating with her mother most of her life. This is common, but parts of Judith's history are unusual. When Judith was born, Oct.29, 1949, her family was launched on a unique career for two decades. Ted and Rita Snow made a remarkable choice, and they were invincible in their commitment to their daughter. Contrary to all medical advice, Judith was never institutionalized. She went to regular schools. Practically, there was no external support at home or in schools. In fact, it was the other extreme. Judith's parents, in addition to being attendants on call 24 hours per day, without holidays, were constantly forced to battle for the opportunity for Judith to be part of the community. When the school system in their original home refused Judith, the whole family packed up and moved to Whitby in 1954. Another move was required to find a high school that would welcome Judith. She registered in Pickering District High School in 1963 and graduated in 1968. The battle was for her survival and it created extraordinary stress. Judith has spent years trying to understand those stresses, and to achieve a kind of peaceful resolution. In Judith's case, I think she has figured it out. I think her insight is profound, and as is often the case, very simple.

When Judith was born, perhaps from the age of two, doctors and the Snow family began to realize that Judith's physical growth was unique. She simply couldn't do many things that other two year olds could do. She became increasingly dependent on her mother and father to take care of the physical needs she was unable to accomplish herself. Thus, from a very early age, Judith had a dual relationship with her family, and her mother in particular. There was the role of mother, but also the role of "attendant". This duality was not identified, acknowledged or understood. But this unique dependence created a different reality for Judith and her parents.

For Judith, there was a gradual and growing awareness of the complexity of her dependence - and therefore, a request/ demand for attendant care so she could function. Since her mother was the primary attendant, there was no distinction drawn between the roles of "loving mother" and attendant. Practically, this meant that if Judith's mother needed a break, or just some time alone - or time to just be Judith's mother, it was twisted into a battle of wits and character - because Judith was frightened that she would be abandoned - and left without support. This war of wits took a toll over the years.

Today, we realize that if we had been able to clarify the two distinct rolls, life might have been much better. The roll of mother included loving, teaching, listening, nurturing and care giving - but not 24 hours per day year after year.

The second and distinct roll was attendant/care giver. If we had been able to separate those functions, Judith's parents could have insisted on time to just be "parents", without having to worry about attendant care for the next 24 hours. They could have asked for the little breaks that we all need, to go to Scottish dancing, to play bridge with some friends, or just to sit quietly and read, or watch the leaves blow. And Judith might not have felt pressured to "demand" that her parents be omnipresent protectors and attendant. But Judith was correctly terrified. There was no attendant care backup. The stress on Rita and Ted was enormous and relentless. There was no acknowledgement of the conflict of roles. So they struggled, irritating each other, trapped in a cocoon with no butterfly in sight.

If they had been able to understand that the situation was crazy making for both of them, they could have enjoyed each other more all these years. But Judith's mother never had time to just be a mother. She was being an attendant first - for decades. And Judith unknowingly, but necessarily felt the resentment of being "the project" - not a daughter. So Judith understood and demanded that her mother be her attendant. She had to. It was a survival strategy. And she resented her mother for never being just "her mother". Over the years, they lived through that tension. Today, I think we can understand it.

Imagine a reality where Judith and her mother could have had a conversation about the overlapping and conflicting rolls of "mother" and "attendant". Judith would have been able to understand then that her mother might just need a break - because she was human. Equally, Judith might need a break. Having another person provide attendant care was not "desertion", but a way of managing reality. Going to Scottish dancing was not abandonment, but a survival strategy, that would actually allow Rita to be a mother. Imagine a world where Rita would have been able to have the support so that occasionally, not all the time, she could just be mother. It would have been a different reality.

And so as we finish this book, we are planning another meeting with Rita and Ted - to talk about our new understanding of the incredible stress they endured, and how their opportunities to be parents were dashed. We want to talk this through with them because after all this time, we have come to realize that our parents did the best possible - the very best they could. Rita and Ted Snow gave their daughter a remarkable foundation so she could be a profound thinker. Building that foundation was very hard work. It was aggravating and crazy making. It was tense and painful. Much of that anguish need not have been. Understanding the contradictory demands placed on the family would have been an enormous contribution, even if there had been no other help. Judith and her mother could have talked through some of the stress. But no one knew. No one acknowledged it. It was just stressful, and it took a toll.

Thank god there is still time to actually share that simple understanding and build and renew a powerful bond between mother and daughter, by understanding the reality they were given.

Equally important, if we can tell this story, perhaps some of the families struggling today can reduce their pain by understanding the complex, confusing and contradictory demands of parenthood when it overlaps with the role of attendant.

Judith talked about this issue:

Now, I realize that there was a much more fundamental issue at stake that neither of us could have understood. The reason I understand it now, is that I have had the opportunity to work with my own attendant care system for over 10 years. One of the issues that constantly comes up in attendant care is the issue of availability. It is essential that the attendant willingly give their mind and their body to the person who is being attended so that person can tell the attendant what it is they want to do, how they want to do it, and thus live and work through the body of that person. If the attendant is unwilling, then the relationship doesn't work. It just falls apart and becomes abusive for both people. In the Joshua Committee, we have to work all the time to be sure the attendants feel free to leave the job, or take time off. We must keep the issue of their availability constantly on the table so they can protect their own willingness to do the job.

With the perspective of that decade of learning, now I realize that at the age of 2 1/2, I needed my own attendant so I could do the things a 2 1/2 year old would do - to live, work and play in my own way. However, my mother and father were my only attendants until I was 19. Neither of us had any choice. Looking back it is clear that this was an abuse to everyone concerned. They were never able to be "unavailable" of their own choice. My mother and father never had the privilege to just be parents. First they had to be attendants - because I had to survive. And I was never allowed to be just Judith. I couldn't risk doing things that a "kid" would want to do - because it could mess up my survival system - my attendant/parents. I never had the choice of working/playing with any one else either. It is a terrible irony. My parents were't allowed to be parents. They had to be attendants - and squeeze in some parenting if there was time. And I was never allowed to be Judith. I had to "manage" my relationship with my attendants, and if there was time to be a daughter or just Judith, maybe it could be fit in. But there was never time.

It is important that parents of today be able to find support and voice their need to have time off and live their own lives. There must be support for their children so they can be in a proper relationship with each other - parent/child. There needs to be space for the child to do whatever he/she needs, and parallel space for the parents so they can have a relationship as a family - and not just as attendants.

Now I really realize the extent which my parents, particularly my mother, created the possibility of my life. I also created the possibility of her life. I became an important identity in her life. She became a warrior. She fought so that I could live and contribute to society. We share that vocation in common, but it was really my mother who created it in the first place.

This is another of the many things that has emerged from this. I can finally see my way past the struggles, to understand how much my parents contributed to my life. That is why Marsha was such a miracle. She broke through all that. There was no place for a Marsha in the world we had created and lived in. No place in the ideas, the language, in my very being for a Marsha. Yet Marsha made it through the wall and created a place for herself.

How did it really happen? It is a mystery. We will never really know. It just happened.

Circles
for the Future

Circles of Friends...

I certainly don't know exactly how all this got started.
Marsha was deeply involved, and so was Judith. I was
preoccupied with Frontier. But somewhere along the line,
Marsha and Judith began to talk about "circles". Since Judith
had started dubbing herself a "portable visionary", I thought
this was just another mirage. But over time, my hard nose
became more pliable and I began to see that this was more
than just words. I also began to understand that I was part of
whatever it was.

The two of them, Marsha and Judith in full flight, was
always a sight. They could generate enough energy to
frighten fusion supporters. But gradually, I saw that this was
more than just intense light. There really was content. The
content was relationships. They both hammered away about
the anguish of being a life long loner. We all need friends

and relationships. It took me a while to comprehend the step
to "circles" - circles of friends. It was simple and profound.
We all have layers of relationships - like concentric circles -
with different levels of intensity in the relationships. What
they discovered was that most people with labels had no
people in their "inner" circles - except perhaps immediate
family. Then their lives were "blank" until you reached the
"outer" circle with "paid people in your life". There, those
with labels had long lists of "caring professionals" who often
had to check the chart to get their name right.

Their vision was ridiculously simple. All one had to do to
improve a person's life was to fill up the inner circles. It
seemed like hocus pocus till you stopped and thought about
putting a few friends in your life. Then it made sense - solid
sense. So they began talking about circles - and how to build
a circle of friends around a person who was lonely. And
suddenly, in one of those blinding glimpses of the obvious, I
realized that I had helped to build a circle of friends around
Judith when she collapsed. We didn't use those words then,
but the Joshua Committee was a circle of friends.

And now, even I talk about circles of friends. It's just
good common sense. Judith and Marsha invented the term.
But I feel rather good, because I was part of the experiment
that moved that dream into reality. I always live events before
I manage to put words around the reality of my life. That is
why it is consistent that I am writing about the Joshua Committee and Circles now - after living it for years. Ironically, now I
understand that I was part of the Joshua Committee from the
beginning. I was there - living it. I was slow to acknowledge
that, but I was there all the time. Marsha knew it right away;
Judith figured it out after a while; I eventually caught on. I
was a lot slower. But now I am trying to recognize and live

my reality more quickly. It's easier for me - and for everyone else. Less confusing. It's one of the little things that Judith has helped me to learn. Judith and I are very similar. It takes us 10 years to recognize the obvious.

There were a thousand reasons that we shouldn't/couldn't trust each other, but we did anyway. Trust doesn't happen quickly. It takes time.

Judith also helped me to see that I am not an island. I too need a circle of friends. This is not something abstract. It is real. And you don't have to wait until everyone is dead or gone. You can do it now.

I have drawn my "circles" now. Fascinating what one sees. Almost all my friends have experience on the "margins" of life. I guess that says something about me.

Planned Spontaneity - From Here to 2000...

We celebrated Judith's 30th birthday party in 1979. We are planning a real bash just before we ring in the millennium together. They said it couldn't be done. What did they know anyway? And besides, we learned, loved and lived a lot. I wouldn't trade a moment of it.

We are embarked on a journey together. This story is not done. We have just established the Centre for Integrated Education and Community. It will grow and present new challenges and opportunities. We are teaching together more. We just completed a week long workshop at Syracuse University, and we are McGill bound. We are a good team - Marsha, Judith and I. And I am still learning from Judith. I am still listening to her talk about "giftedness" in my head. I

116

am comfortable with the notion that we all have "gifts", but it is yet another leap to see "presence" as a gift. I am learning. Judith is teaching. We are doing it together.

And we all continue to explore new worlds. One of Judith's dreams was to be a "rock star" - in a rock video. We all knew it was ridiculous, but the impossible is only hard work for Judith. "Labelling Blues", a rock video by Greg Hoskins and the Stick People, with Judith in it, is just being released.

And the circles interlock again and again. Appropriately for renewed beginnings, Judith has just joined her Church choir. After 20 years of hiding behind the piano, she is coming out again.

As for me, I have realized at long last that Judith is part of my Circle of Friends. We have come full circle. We circled around Judith in 1979, and now, she has circles around us. Who could have foreseen?

We went canoeing again - in the brisk fall waters of the Madawaska River. Marsha was terrified that Judith would get hypothermia. I said "That's the wrong problem. If we flip, not drowning will be the first priority". Marsha refocused her fear, turned it into an opportunity and recorded our adventure in slides. They are wonderful. So were the fall colours. We didn't run any rapids. We just went canoeing. If there was ever any doubt in my mind about the "dignity of risk", all I had to do was bask in the glow from Judith's face.

Later she said, "I was a little scared about drowning, but then I thought - what a way to go. It was so beautiful". Marsha cooked a celebration dinner, and we toasted life as the coals glowed red in the wood stove.

And now we sit at the Kowloon Restaurant editing this article. We are celebrating our course in Syracuse and the success of the Summer Institute at McGill. We are looking forward to taking our "Institute" - the Centre - on the road. We just ordered Judith's first passport. World here we come.

Most important, we are relishing every moment of life as we reflect and dream with planned spontaneity for a celebration of friendship to ring in the year 2000 - together.

More later...

Nov. 24, 1990: Late Breaking Update;

Following a memorial tribute to Father Patrick Mackan, delivered by Marsha and I at the Frontier College Annual Meeting this morning, Judith Snow was elected to the Board of Governors of the College. Virtually the first act of the new Chair of the Board, Dr. Gary Bunch, was to ask Judith to organize a memorial for Patrick Mackan, jointly with the Centre for Integrated Education and Community. In the Board Meeting in the afternoon, Judith was appointed to the search committee to select my successor as President. The circle continues...

Afterword...

Reflections on Jack's Story of Judith and Her Companions*

John O'Brien

Hasidic teachers say, "God created people because God loves stories." If they teach truly, the creator delights in the story woven from the lives of Judith and Marsha and Jack and their friends. Their story sobers, instructs, and nourishes hope.

Jack's story of Judith sobers because it asks us to face facts in their lives that challenge some comfortable beliefs.

• It comforts to believe in the meticulous professionalism that reaches its peak in hospital operating theaters. It sobers to recognize that, even with vigilant friends, Judith's throat was scarred by one of the best trained people in the world who, unobservant and unthinking, pushed the wrong breathing tube too hard.

---

* Preparation of this chapter was supported through a subcontract from The Center on Human Policy, Syracuse University for the Research & Training Center on Community Living. The Research & Training Center on Community living is supported through a cooperative agreement (Number H133B80048) between the National Institute on Disability & Rehabilitation Research (NIDRR) and the University of Minnesota Institute on Community Integration. Members of the Center are encouraged to express their opinions; these do not necessarily represent the official position of NIDRR.

• It comforts to believe that there are solutions for people with disabilities and that the only problems are getting enough resources to produce them. If only there were enough residential places or enough home health agencies to provide well trained attendants or enough Joshua committees, then people with disabilities would be taken care of for life. It sobers to notice how unpredictably things have changed in Judith's life as she discovers more of herself, as new resources become available, and as she and her circle learn from experience what works for her and what doesn't. Freezing the arrangements of any moment in the story into Judith's "lifeplan" or "perfect placement" would kill her story from the inside out.

• It comforts to believe that people with disabilities will be able to change unjust situations alone, by speaking up for themselves. It sobers to realize that –even after successfully organizing a major change in her province's policy– Judith, as articulate and assertive a person as ever I have met, still relies on her circle of friends to survive everyday living and to hold in place her lifeline system of personal assistants.

• It comforts to believe in good organizations. Not many perhaps, but at least a few social systems that fully embody human values and thus can be trusted to care. It is disappointing, though not surprising, to be reminded that public agencies charged with caring will only fund tailor made support for an individual if she and her friends remain highly skilled at personally influencing people with power to bend the rules. But it is sobering to find that even a small voluntary organization, committed to social change throughout its distinguished history and led by Judith's friends, could come to a point of organizational crisis that threatened Judith, even momentarily.

• It comforts to believe in good people who will, if asked and supported, generously do the everyday work of caring without thought of compensation. It sobers to acknowledge that Judith cannot be who she is without employing several people who have good jobs at decent pay, and that the task of coordinating her system of personal assistance competes with her work and adds to her anxiety unless someone else shares responsibility for it.

• It comforts to believe that most people with disabilities are well looked after and Judith simply fell through the system's cracks, because she is unusually gifted. It is sobering to consider that all people – including all people with disabilities– have unique and beautiful gifts, as Judith does. What makes Judith an exception is not her giftedness but her destiny. She comes to the world with the vision, energy, and charm to attract and organize able people who have found rewards in her friendship and meaning in their shared struggle for personal and social change. It is frightening to imagine the lives of isolated people whose gifts – as real as Judith's but more quiet– wait for discovery by a circle of friends who will work together to develop them.

This powerful story may be too much to digest. When the news contradicts comfortable beliefs, it's tempting to ignore the news, perhaps by finding reasons to discount the message. Reasons like these may come to mind:

"She wants too much; she should accept her disability."

"She's too dependent on her friends; she should be more independent in advocating for herself (maybe with the help of a lawyer) and in managing her personal assistance system (maybe with the help of professionals with disabilities)."

"She's just creating an individual exception inside a corrupt system; she should pursue a collective solution that will overturn the corrupt system."

"She put her trust in an organization, what else can she expect but trouble; she should believe more strongly in people's goodness."

"She is unique, a hero surrounded by heroes; no ordinary people could expect to live as she and her friends do."

Maybe each of these responses fit some other person's life. But they cannot validly be presented as true for all people with a disability. They don't match the complex, confusing, exciting reality of Judith's circumstances as she and her friends live them.

Jack's story of Judith instructs because Judith and Marsha trust him to tell us about their lives together. Judith, or Marsha, or another member of the Joshua Committee would tell their story differently. Jack's telling, in writing and during a long absence from Judith, grows from his need to take stock of his own life. He writes first for himself, then, with Judith's permission, for us. His version of Judith's story gives us the point of view of someone deeply personally engaged, who took the role of strategist, task organizer, and administrative and practical fixer in most of the events he describes. It is Jack who will think to bring lots of rope along on the Diamond Club soiree. Allowed backstage, we hear some of the craft secrets of a group of talented advocates, three of whom become the closest of friends, as they learn to make lunch a life changing experience for senior bureaucrats. Allowed to overhear Jack's memories of turning points in his friendship, we learn something of the struggle and rewards of slowly coming to greater trust. These turns don't leave anyone's sense of correctness or administrative cool intact – imagine throwing a friend out on Christmas – but no friendship deepens without cracking through its own accumulated expectations. Along the way, we hear a little bit about some of the social inventions energized by the relationships among Judith and Marsha and Jack and their friends. We learn of circles of friends, integration action groups, new ways to teach apprentice physicians, and new forms of personal assistance with new policies to fund them.

Jack's story of Judith teaches by catching us in a paradox. Jack repeats, "This is not about disability." But he tells of a person who cannot make or drink a cup of tea without assistance and who, along with her friends, must remain continually vigilant to protect against the negative effects of a social structure designed to exile people with disability. And he writes matter of factly about lifting Judith, dealing with inaccessible buildings, assisting with meals, and scheming to change provincial disability policy. So how can this be anything but a story about disability? Maybe because the questions disability raises can never be answered well as long as they are taken up at the level of disability. Maybe creative responses have to arise from a deeply shared perception that Judith's concerns are human concerns. She reminds us that if we fall into fixing or remediating a disabled person, we fall short of working with her to build a more just, more caring community. What's good for Judith is good for all of us. What's good for Judith does not come because of, or in spite of her disability, but because of who she is, in the body she has.

Jack's story of Judith nourishes hope because it chronicles 12 years of companionship. It is the story of a company in the oldest sense of the word. Jack catches this sense of the word company in his frequent reference to meals. Long before it was a legal form for doing business, a company was a group of people who shared their daily bread (pan). The root meaning embodied in the word company (pa), and in this

story of companionship, is nourishment and mutual
protection.

In company –out of shared meals and shared work– Jack
and Judith's friendship slowly grew. In a day when digital
watches make us aware of the press of seconds passing and
anxious for rapid culminations, there is hope in attending to
the order of things here: first company, then, more slowly,
friendship. We don't have to be friends all at once. We don't
have to trip ourselves up trying to will something that only
comes spontaneously. It's enough for us to choose to faith-
fully share daily work and daily bread.

At a time when many people take community as synony-
mous with a peak feeling of intimacy (which cannot be
sustained under the pressures of daily life), there is hope in
discovering deep and lasting bonds among companions who
confess to discomfort in sharing all that they feel and to
dealing with their Christmas crisis by avoiding one another
for several months and then finding excuses to talk about
something else in order to renew their relationship.

When much of our shared consciousness focuses on the
achievements of individuals pursuing their own desires no
matter what, awareness of the ties of belonging to others fade
into shadow. There is hope in contemplating a story whose
hero can only pursue her quest for individual fulfillment if
she belongs to a company of adventurers who allow her to
lead them for a significant part of their lives.

There is reason for hope if we can learn some of the
practical lessons of this story.

• Companionship can grow from joint projects, even
projects as ephemeral as planning a conference, if the process
brings people together around their dreams and if the process
includes sharing everyday tasks like eating and helping

another to eat.

• Companions easily mistake partial knowledge for complete understanding. Think about Jack's lack of awareness of the two worlds Judith lived in while she was in the chronic care hospital. She showed and he saw the competence and light in her daytime life. She went nightly into abuse and helplessness. Think about how long it took for Judith and Jack to understand that what Judith felt as abandonment, Jack saw as exciting news. Listening isn't easy; it's hard.

• Serious problems, even personal collapse need not end in disaster. Personal collapse becomes turning point if the person who can't go on asks for help from her companions and if her companions can discover the resources among themselves to face the changes required. Think about Judith's giving up to Peter. Think about Judith's companions gathering to face the fundamental question she posed in her withdrawal: do we want Judith in the world with us and what are we willing to do to keep her here? Facing this question organized the resources they shared in a new, more powerful way.

• People don't need to be perfect to form a strong company. Arguments and ego and anger and disappointment and saying 'I told you so" and pulling away and being afraid make this a human story rather than a technical assistance manual. What it takes to be a strong company is not perfection but fidelity: the willingness to give what each member can and to stay together (or get back together) and keep on together.

• It's not over with the first victory. Facing continuing outside threats to Judith's survival strengthens the company's skills. Living consciously with the ambiguity of resources that fall far short of fully supporting reasonable expectations creates tension. Funding has never been sufficient for the amount of personal assistance Judith needs. Even the new provincial policy requires organizations to administer funds for people rather than offering people the option of managing cash for themselves. If the company deals with these tensions by actively searching for ever better approximations of what is desirable, they grow stronger. If they fall into ignoring problems or into unproductive argument with one another, they grow weaker and Judith becomes more vulnerable.

• Everybody needs the support of companions. As life raises the specter of cancer, the loss of a job, conflict and danger at work, people can turn to one another to deepen and strengthen friendship. And so the company grows stronger.

• Individual development continues as trust grows between companions and as the shared pursuit of individual dreams in the face of opposition creates changes. One sign of growing strength is increasing willingness to discover guidance in images from within one's self. Think about Judith recovering and sharing the painful memory of putting herself behind the piano and stilling her singing. Once shared, this painful memory strengthens relationships and then translates into new action: joining her church choir.

Burton Blatt once wrote of the sort of hope this story nourishes. He said,

> *Optimism is not in believing that*
> *things will turn out well, objectively,*
> *But in believing that we can face things,*
> *subjectively, however they turn out.*
> *Optimism is not in feeling good,*
> *But in feeling that good has a chance to survive.*

127

> *Optimism flows not from defeats*
> *and bitterness or victories and joys of the past,*
> *But in being here now, knowing*
> *the past has strengthened you.*

If he could read Jack's story of Judith, I think he would find his conviction alive and growing.

Appendix 1-A

BRADWIN ADDRESS

89th Annual Meeting
Frontier College
Oct. 22, 1988

Judith A. Snow, M.A.

It is an honour to be invited to give the Bradwin Address at the 89th Annual General Meeting of Frontier College. I consider it a great distinction to be numbered among those eminent people who have given this address in the past. Frontier College has a history of being, and can continue to be I believe, an agent of social good in our nation. I hope that my words today will foster this capacity of our venerable College to bring about a better world.

There are a number of reasons, I suspect, why I would be chosen to give this talk this year. For one thing, I am obviously a member of a group of people who have been pushed out to the margins of our society. I say "obviously" somewhat tongue-in-cheek for in fact I am unusual among disabled people. I have a job, I live in my own home, I have been able to avoid ongoing poverty, I have a good education and I have a large network of friends, colleagues, and even a husband. Frontier College has had a great deal to do with these accomplishments, and I will speak more of this later. But I have lived on the margins, and have fought hard to become a participating citizen. It is an experience worth speaking about.

Another reason for choosing me is that I have thought a lot about what it takes to make real community for people. I am a thinker and a dreamer, and I have been watching the people around me. I have gathered something of a reputation for being a visionary, and today I want to explore one expression of this vision. Let's look at what fosters community; community capable of meeting the needs of all people in all their diversity.

There is a theme that has nurtured my pondering for a number of years. This theme is found in an ancient scriptural passage which is dear to both Jews and Christians. It was written by disciples of Isaiah at a time when Israel was struggling with political humiliation and social crisis. It was quoted by Jesus as a way of announcing his mission of spiritual liberation. I am taking this passage from the Jerusalem Bible.

> *The Spirit Of Yahweh Has Been Given To Me, For Yahweh Has Anointed Me. He Has Sent Me To Bring Good News To The Poor, To Bind Up Hearts That Are Broken;*
>
> *To Proclaim Liberty To Captives, Freedom To Those In Prison; To Proclaim A Year Of Favour From Yahweh, A Day Of Vengeance For Our God,*
>
> *To Comfort All Those Who Mourn And To Give Them For Ashes A Garland; For Mourning Robes The Oil Of Gladness, For Despondency, Praise They Are To Be Called "Terebinths Of Integrity," Planted By Yahweh To Glorify Him.*
>
> *They Will Rebuild The Ancient Ruins, They Will Raise What Has Long Lain Waste, They Will Restore The Ruined Cities, All That Has Lain Waste For Ages PAST.*

This passage, found in Isaiah 61, verses 1-4, speaks about how those who are members of society, and those who are marginalized from society, have a great need for each other's gifts. We are told that when the captives are liberated, and when the poor have heard the good news, they will rebuild the ancient ruins and restore the places that have been devastated.

This need for each other is not perfectly obvious. On the one hand those who are on the margin are usually there for very good reasons. Society often cannot respond smoothly to these people and their needs. Perhaps the physical environment is an obstacle to a person, and he or she is seen as physically handicapped. Perhaps this one has not learned as quickly or as well as others, or perhaps he or she is more active, or more impulsive, or more curious than most folks, and so he or she is seen as impaired in mind, or as a criminal, or as just simply dangerous. In any case the presence of this person disrupts the flow of things as they are, and makes ordinary activity and daily decisions difficult to carry out. The margin may be a dangerous place, but at least there you know who you are, and you are not constantly facing disapproval and discomfort.

On the other hand there is the "ordinary" citizen who fits in, who learns, who knows the ropes and how to swing on them. In this there is peace and protection from challenge. Why would the members of these two groups what to have anything to do with each other when this can only disrupt a workable system?

The passage from Isaiah gives us the eternal answer, although the answer calls forth other questions. Without welcoming the gifts of the stranger, society is doomed to slowly crumble under the weight of its own inertia.

It is certainly clear that breakdown is happening in every part of our world today. Everywhere the numbers of people

who live in the streets and in the prisons increase, and everywhere children swell the ranks of these homeless ones,
because they see no future in school or in work for themselves.
Our environment is degraded to the point where its own
healing powers may not be able to cope with the damage even
if we were to stop despoiling our planet today. Other crises
abound, so much so that there is a great temptation to bury
one's head in the sand.

The sand of ordinary life if lived in community where
people spend their days doing very ordinary things. They
write, talk on telephones, teach children, play with babies,
wash dishes, go for walks, read books, and cry on each
other's shoulders. All of this happens in ordinary places on
commonplace streets, all the time, everywhere. This very
commonness is a real gift, a real benefit not to be ignored. It
is perfectly understandable that we should want to protect our
ordinary lives from the kind of change that crisis and the
stranger threaten to force on us. And that desire to lose
oneself in everyday activity is real, for don't we all long for a
peaceful and ordinary life? What do we know about dealing
with these over-whelming problems?

But change comes whether we are prepared for it or not. If
we are to cope with the challenge of crisis then we need the
gift of changing. this gift is not to be found among ordinary
people; ordinary people have the gift of everydayness.

The gift of surviving and growing through change belongs
to the outcast. Ancient writings tell us this and modern
experience confirms it. Living on the edge of chaos changes
the people who survive it. You become very aware of the
value of things ordinary citizens take for granted; things like
having your opinion listened to, having a chance to make a
mistake, to be forgiven and to have a chance to try again;

things like having friends and family who celebrate holidays with you and who will tell their friends that you are looking for a job. Living on the margin either burns you out and kills you, or it turns you into a dreamer, someone who really knows what sort of change will help and who can just about taste it; someone who is prepared to do anything to bring about change. If these dreamers are liberated, if they are brought back into the arms of society, they become the architects of the new community; a community that has a new capacity to support everyone's needs and interactions. But how can this really be, especially since these dreamers still have the characteristics that marked them as outcasts in the first place? They will still lack good judgement, or find it hard to learn to read, or be disabled. Solving this problem is critical, for otherwise the outcasts and the ordinaries are very good at maintaining an invisible wall between their two worlds.

This reminds me of certain parties I was invited to when I was a child. Once a year some group would put on a party and invite all the disabled children and their parents. This would always include a turkey dinner or hot dogs and ice cream, and each child would always get a present. At other times these same people would raise money to buy equipment or send us off to the camp for "crippled" children. I sometimes wonder if those men hated the parties as much as we did, especially after we got to be ten years old or so. Our parents wanted us to go because they depended on their charity to meet our extraordinary needs, but we always knew that these people were not a real part of our lives, and that they didn't really want to know us as friends. Otherwise I could have gone to camp with their sons and daughters, and I could have visited some of them at their homes, and they would have

visited mine. As it was, we never got to see each other as real
people, nor did they ever get to see me as real.

No, for the citizen and the outcast to come together, to
dream and work together, to rebuild community together,
something different must happen. This difference depends
upon the quality of the relationship built between the one who
is reaching out and the one who is reaching in.

There usually comes a time in the lives of people who are
living on the margin when they are prepared to risk giving up
their identities as outcasts to try to become participating
citizens of community. For an ex-offender it might be a
moment of finally wanting to go straight, to get a job; for the
disabled person it might come as a time of wanting to move
out of a group home, to get a job. For me it came nine years
ago this month when I was living in a chronic care hospital
not far from here. I use the term "living" loosely because in
fact I was dying from a combination of malnutrition, overdoses
of prescribed drugs, and a sense of hopelessness born from
ten years of fighting without success to get needed attendant
care. From my earliest childhood, doctors had told me that I
could not live to see my 30th birthday, and nine years ago,
weeks away from that day, I figured that my days were
numbered. And I was angry. I was prepared to work hard at
living my own life, and I was prepared to help others where I
could, but I was still looking for the break that I needed to be
able to really become myself. I decided that living inside the
hospital and trying to survive outside it were about equal risks
for me. I moved out. Five months later I was still alive, but
all my resources ran out and I collapsed. I could have ended
up back in the hospital or I might have tried suicide, but
something fundamental had changed in my life during that
year, and so I can tell you a different story.

I had friends. One woman had reached out to me while I was still in the hospital. She used to do things like share meals with me, invite me to her home, ask me to help her in a variety of ways, and work with me on different projects. For months I didn't know how to respond to her because I didn't know what a friend was, but eventually I opened up to her and we have become very close. While I was in the hospital and in the months before my collapse, she was introducing me to her friends and family and telling them how we worked together, not how unfortunate I was to be so different. Her husband built a ramp on their house so that I could enter with ease. As friends together we celebrated my 30th birthday.

Then my collapse happened, friends took me to her house. She called together 14 of our friends and colleagues and they worked out a plan to get me back to work, back to life, back to fighting trim again. Within six days I was living in a new apartment of my own, with a full staff of attendants, with a loan to pay their salaries, and I was back at work. Then we sat down together to work out a way to get the government to pay for this real service. Within three months we had the first contract in Canada for an individually funded attendant care programme. We had to find an agency to channel the contract, since the government is unable to give funding directly to an individual. We approached Frontier College to perform this role and Frontier said "Yes". Frontier is still my agent.

Today there are hundreds of individually funded arrangements across Canada, standing as a witness to what will be the ordinary way to fund attendant care some day. But my support group achieved the first one. I call this group the Joshua Committee, and of course, Jack Pearpoint, Marsha Forest and I were the founders of the Joshua Committee.

Clearly that is not the end of the story. The Joshua

Committee continues to play a very important role in my life. During the first year of working together there was a lot of yelling on all sides. After all we came from different sides of the picture, and we didn't know how to trust and listen to each other. I had a lot of growing and changing to do to make up for years of lack of opportunity and of living up to the definition of myself as being disabled. On the other hand, the other members of the Joshua Committee had no reason to believe that I could live the way I thought I could, or that my dreams were based on my real gifts. We had to learn to be bound by each others dreams, abilities, and limitations. We had to be community for each other. One other lesson had to be learned. This is a lesson that I have seen others struggle with as well. Ordinary citizens seem to believe that once a person has been brought into community with the initial problems solved, things will continue along just fine. It seems easy to forget that even though we undoubtedly have gifts, there still is a pressure that pushes us toward the margin again. In my case people will always see me as severely disabled no matter what I do or become. This expresses itself now and then as some government official deciding that it is time for me to go back to the hospital. Then my contract for attendant care doesn't get renewed. Once this happened about six years ago when the Joshua Committee hadn't met for several months, and we were deep into a crisis before we all could work together well again. For true community building to take root, the stranger and the citizens have to make a permanent commitment to each other; one that may change in form several times but that continues with fulfilling interaction on all parts.

Frontier College has participated in a number of formal and not so formal commitments, that have welcomed strangers in from the margins of society. Frontier/Beat the Street draws on what street kids already know and care about to liberate their minds and their will to become à creative part of society. Frontier/HELP depends on the smarts, the dogged perseverance and the vision of people who have been literal outlaws. In fact from the very beginning Frontier College has welcomed the stranger in the one who could not read, so that he or she could participate, making Canada a stronger place to be. The board, members, volunteers, staff and friends of Frontier College have understood what it takes to be true liberators. She has stayed strong through building a continuing relationship with the very people she has welcomed in.

Frontier College is now eighty-nine years old. I believe that as the dust settles others will look to Frontier College as a model of how to build creative organizations in the communities of the future. Her strength comes from her tradition of allying herself with the dreamers on the edge. My hope is that this kind of partnership will continue to be the heart of the College in the future. I am confident that it will.

Happy 89th Birthday Frontier College

Judith Snow

Appendix 1-B

A Medical Introduction to Judith Snow

On Oct. 29, 1990, her forty first birthday, Judith Snow summerized her medical conditions as follows:

* Congenital progressive atrophy of the skeletal muscles due to Spinal Muscular Atrophy. It has been in remission since 1978 leaving compete quadriplegia with full bowel and bladder function. There is low power and limited range of motion in right thumb, but no other power or range of motion in limbs. (permanent condition)

* Significant loss of cranial nerve function including Horner's syndrome in left eye. Some difficulty in swallowing due to Horner's and diverticulosis of esophagus. (Permanent condition)

* Limited mandible motion and enlarged tongue with spasticity typical of spinal muscular atrophy. (Permanent Condition)

* Inguinal hernia - repaired left side at age 1.

* Hiatus Hernia - 1970 (ongoing)

* Harrington Instrumentation - 1972 - for severe Scoliosis. Resulted in semi-paralysis of left side of body. Lost use of left hand. Temporary paralysis of right hand - recovered partially. By 1976, right hand totally paralysed except for minimal movement in thumb.

* Spinal fusion from C5 to S1 - 1972

* Bilateral Girdle stone. (removed hip joints) - 1972. Repeat of procedure in 1988.

* Some arthritis in knees and right shoulder due to lack of muscular support for the joints.

* Sleep apnea (approximately 26% of typical air volume for age) corrected with a Continuous Positive Air Pressure (CPAP) ventilator at night.

* Non infectious, non-viral hepatitis in remission.

* Inflammation of both kidneys - under control by medication.

* Irregular menses due to radiation to both ovaries at age 12.

* Allergies - sodium benzoate and sulfa drugs and other food dies.

* Osteoporosis - (decalcification, softening of bones due to lack of weight bearing).

* A tendency to oedema, (water retention).

Judith summed it up.

"I'm a definite candidate for chronic care. Any two of my eight conditions would qualify me to live out my days in a geriatric ward."

"But I won't."

* * * * * * * *

ABOUT THE AUTHOR

After graduating from the University of
Saskatchewan in 1968, Jack Pearpoint left
Canada for 5 years with CUSO in West Africa.
He became President of Frontier College,
Canada's oldest adult education organization in
1975. For 15 years, Jack has been a leader in the
international literacy movement. He is a lecturer,
writer and administrator in building inclusive
communities where "all belong". He devotes his
life and work to building a more just and demo-
cratic society. Jack is a Director of the Centre for
Integrated Education and Community the
President of Inclusion Press International. He
travels the world with his colleague and wife, Dr.
Marsha Forest, providing training events in tools
for change. He is interested in your comments
and reactions. Write c/o

Inclusion Press International,
24 Thome Crescent,
Toronto, Ontario. M6H-2S5.
Tel: 416-658-5363),
Fax: 416-658-5067
WEB Page: http://inclusion.com

Marsha, Sheldon, Judith, TeRipowai & Jack at Garden Avenue house (1997)

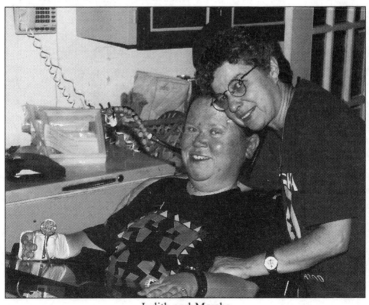

Judith and Marsha

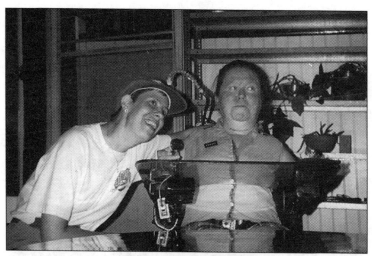
Miriam and her friend, Judith

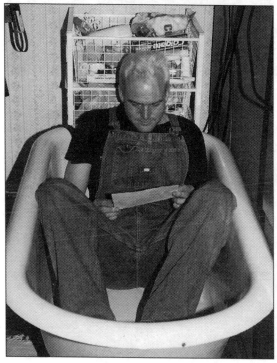
Sheldon in the
Garden Avenue
reading room

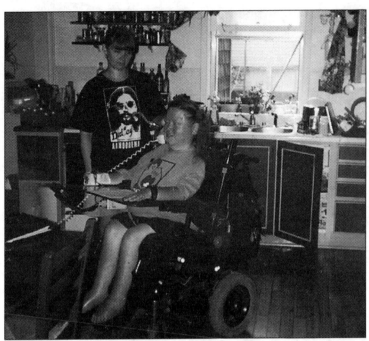

Judith cooking in the kitchen

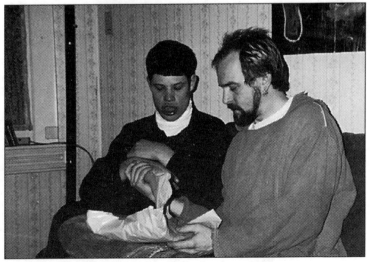

Matt and Sheldon at Garden Avenue house

Judith at Stonehenge in England

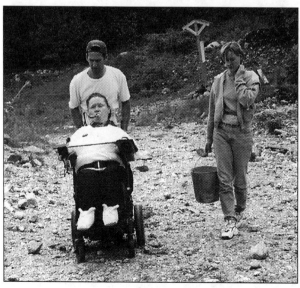

Judith digging in the Rose Quartz quarry

Judith and Jack, in England, on the canals

Judith swimming with Jay Klein

Judith on the fly

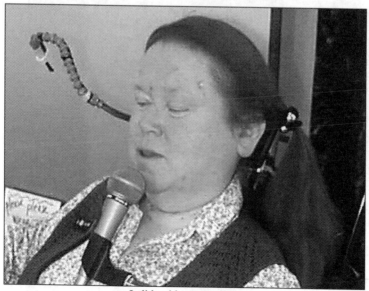

Judith mid-presentation

Shafik Asante & Judith at the Toronto Summer Institute, 1997

Judith canoeing

Judith and Jack canoeing

WHAT'S REALLY WORTH DOING AND HOW TO DO IT

A Book for People Who Love Someone Labeled Disabled

(Possibly Yourself)

JUDITH A. SNOW

INCLUSION PRESS

Introduction

by

John McKnight

This book is the wisdom of a woman who has been 44 years among us. It is a humbling book, because it makes me feel, at 62, as though I have been living in slow motion. How has she managed to do so much that she knows this much in only 44 years?

For anyone who has been near Judith, the answer is obvious for she burns so brightly. And this illumination lights her way through unexpected places.

In this book, you can follow the path she has explored. It is not a path cut through forests or forged across prairies. It is not a path won by feats over nature. Instead, it is a path created by nurture.

Judith's way is opened by dreaming. Along the way, gifted lives joined the journey. And when she finally arrives we see her dancing.

This book is Judith's invitation to join in the dance of life. She is graceful and lovely as she lights our lives and leads the way. You will never forget the joy and celebration of Judith's journey if you join her. And in the end, she will have led you out of disability into community.

John McKnight

John McKnight is a professor at North Western University in Chicago. He is a good friend of Judith and the Centre.

WHY THIS BOOK AND WHY NOW

Since 1980 my Joshua Committee and I have become famous in the English speaking world — and in a few places beyond. With the publication of **From Behind the Piano — the Building of Judith Snow's Unique Circle of Friends**, (Jack Pearpoint, Inclusion Press, Toronto, 1990), the concepts of relationship building and inclusive participation took root and grew everywhere. Together with many friends internationally we were discovering that the key to building supportive relationships and Inclusion is understanding 'Giftedness'. The power of Inclusion and Giftedness are the impetus of this growth and the inspiration of this book.

My closest colleagues and I have worked over time to develop the ideas and strategies of Inclusion and Giftedness. We are working to counteract the limitations that society everywhere imposes on those considered to be disabled. I was asked to collect these ideas and some of the stories together. The purpose of this work is to describe the building of community and participation around the very people who are so often rejected and who are almost inevitably perceived as limited in their contributions to our world. For me it is an adventure and a pleasure to create this book.

I want to thank the Georgia Advocacy Office for making the writing and publication of this book possible. The work of building Inclusion as a philosophy and guideline for being with vulnerable people is not done sitting at a desk nine to five. I have lived on grants and from consulting jobs for 14 years, striving to follow the paths that labeled people lay out for me in their lives and dreams. I could not have discovered my own or others' insights about community nearly as deeply if I had had to work on a typical career. The generosity of the Georgia Advocacy Office in supporting me to write these words allows me to draw my thoughts and experience together. I hope that the result of this effort also benefits you, the reader.

For me this is essentially a book about how to live well. Knowing how to appreciate and support the participation of and contributions from people who society typically rejects is part of living well.

This is a book inspired by:

- people labeled disabled,

- others vulnerable to rejection, and

- those who love them.

Its writing comes from my personal experience and my reflections on the lives and doings of many people around me and before me. It is my fundamental belief that no true, lasting community can be built without the gifts of people vulnerable to exclusion.

This work can also be read as a book of strategies — hence its name. People labeled disabled and others with similar experience would be badly served by a bunch of baseless, theoretical ideas with no practical application. Be sure that this book is meant to be used to help the reader find a different angle from which to solve a problem and to discover a variety of truly useful ways of building a support structure — one that will make it possible for you and perhaps someone you love to be more present, more powerful and more appreciated in a community you can choose.

158

Beginning with my parents, Ted and Rita Snow, and with Marsha Forest and Jack Pearpoint many hundreds of people have smoothed my life path. They make it possible for me to choose my life, to belong and not be alone, to love and be loved, and to make a difference. In the end there is nothing more important. I thank you all.

I type with my mouth using a breath operated Morse Code system. Needless to say I was glad when other, more able typists took over some of this labour. I thank Mimi, Pat, Savoy and Ian, all personal assistants of mine, for their willing work.

John McKnight not only introduces this book but his love and understanding of community are also part of this writing. John has taught us all about the devastation that human services have wreaked on the world of supportive and loving relationships. I write as a colleague and friend of John McKnight, determined to create a bulwark around human community wherever possible.

About Mike

One other man deserves a heartfelt acknowledgment and thank you — Mike Green. I met Mike at the McGill Summer Institute on Integrated Education and Community. I teach in the two week Foundations of Inclusion course there every year along with Marsha, Jack and John O'Brien. (By the way, John helped arrange for the funding to write this book.) Mike was a student at McGill in 1993. He was inspired to attend by people who were designing the Inclusive classroom where his daughter, Annie, is a student.

Before our class was concluded, Mike had already signed up for a four day intensive workshop called **Hand In Hand**. The following October, Martha Leary and I co-facilitated this ground breaking seminar on communication and supportive relationship. In the intervening months Mike wrote weekly or oftener. He stayed at my place during **Hand in Hand**.

As Mike listened deeply, made career changes to line up his personal life with Inclusion, brought Inclusion to the 'mental health' arena — as he inspired countless people in a few short months to examine this new possibility — I was deeply moved by his understanding, commitment, insight, spirituality and love.

As I started to write this book I was struggling deeply. Then I realized — I never do anything alone and **Giftedness** is all about meaningful interaction. Why was I trying to write this book as an 'I'? I invited Mike to write with me.

For five days Mike listened, typed with one finger, cooked, shopped, walked dogs, took notes and generally did what it took to get this book nearly written in a five day marathon. His inspiration, work and love run through this writing like the blood in my veins. Eventually Mike consented to have his words stand on their own. They are marked specifically in the text.

I bring this book with all my heart. enjoy.

 Judtih A. Snow

THE BEGINNING:
DISABILITY

A paradigm is a set of ideas and assumptions that we think through. It is like a lens -- an object that we look through. Just as one lens gives one view of the world and another lens gives a different view so different paradigms give people different ways of thinking about the world.

Galileo discovered a way of putting certain lenses together that made planets and stars appear in ways that were never possible before. His new tool — a telescope — gave rise to a lot of controversy and conflict. On the heels of this friction came a great revolution in theology, in human liberation and ability, in knowledge and understanding.

But Galileo had to be able to imagine a telescope. He had to be able to have the new thought called "telescope". He had to be able to realize that creating a telescope would help him prove that the planets and stars were in a different relationship with our earth than previously understood. Otherwise why would he take the trouble to invent a telescope? Or, if he had stumbled across the invention, why wouldn't he just use it to look down the street?

This new thought came because of a shift of paradigms going on among people of his day — one that was causing many folks to challenge the then current ideas about who God was and who men and women were. People were sensing different possibilities in themselves and in their society and went looking for different evidence to back up their experience. They changed their paradigm and the new paradigm changed the world.

Why is this important? Why start looking for ways to support people in the community by thinking about Galileo? Well maybe — just maybe — the problem we are facing in supporting vulnerable people to have vibrant lives filled with friendship, vitality and activity is not that we aren't doing enough or that we need a better plan and more money. Maybe we, as a whole culture, are doing the wrong think. (Yes, I mean think.)

Disability is a paradigm. Believing in disability allows us to have certain thoughts and assumptions about people. The whole notion of disability depends on the thought that people can be hampered by limitations.

The disability paradigm sends us looking for limitations in some people's minds and bodies. For example every child in North America for at least the last 50 years has had his or her 'IQ' tested. We do this because we believe (think it is real) that some people's minds are functioning inadequately.

When we discover the limitations we were looking for, we seek ways to contain or eliminate them. If a child is discovered to have an 'IQ' below 85, people will recommend tutoring, counselling, perhaps medical testing and treatment. If these efforts are unsuccessful we try to disguise or accommodate the limitations. The child with the lower 'IQ' will typically be streamed into special education.

Our feelings and emotions are another area of our lives which is more and more determined by our search for limitations. Psychiatrists and other medical practitioners have taken ownership of our moods and emotions. They are following the direction of a culture that says that happiness is our correct condition and that sadness or anger are limitations on feeling good. More and more designer drugs are being developed to

162

change doubt into confidence and depression into mellowness. Even a mellow mood can be chemically altered into exuberance.

The paradigm of disability affects every part of our lives. It teaches us that where we should look for our abilities is in our own selves and bodies. Our certainty that disability exists affects how we raise and spend public dollars. It affects the status, employment, income and marriageability of people — to name a partial list. It affects who can and does ride the bus. Belief in disability affects who does or does not get to be born and the grace with which we approach our advancing years. Disability is a fundamental paradigm determining in part each day of everybody's lives.

The paradigm of disability looks at limitations and teaches us to go and find ways of overcoming them.

When we first examine this paradigm it seems positive and powerful. What we don't see at first is its incredible cost. This foremost cost is that we have all become mesmerized by our supposed limitations. **We have become certain that only young, happy and otherwise perfect people are eligible for fulfilment. Until we attain these three conditions we consider ourselves wounded in our ability to be creative or to make a contribution.**

Mike: As a society we are frightened of human vulnerability. Our society battles hopelessly against change. Stay young, stay happy, stay in love, stay prosperous, stay, stay, stay. If it won't stay we try to fix it, or forget it. We do not easily accept that life is change and that a normal part of life as change is aging, sickness, even death, as well as youth, wellness and life. This anxiety and fear of accepting and supporting life as

163

> *it is leads to a drive to fix each other or abandon one*
> *another rather than see each other's vulnerability*
> *and support one another to be who and how we are.*

There is more than an individual cost in the disability paradigm. Many of us have taken on roles in the world of helping others to overcome their limitations. Our efforts are continually frustrated since limitations are inherent in all of life. Frustration builds upon frustration as we can neither perfect the person we are assisting nor perfect our own ability to overcome limitation. We become trapped in a frenzy of unfulfillment.

On top of this, limitations upset us as a society, especially in a democracy. We understand that people must have access to choices, opportunities and options. We know that if people exercise this access they will grow in their relationships, skills, knowledge, judgment and experience. In turn they will have more to offer in community. This creates more options, choice and opportunity, and everyone benefits.

Now we 'know' that if someone doesn't walk, doesn't speak, doesn't see or hear, doesn't know how to put their trousers on the right way or doesn't understand socially acceptable behaviour that these circumstances will create limitations in their lives. It is true that I cannot move my arms and legs and that that means I cannot get from one side of the room to the other by myself and that can mean a very restricted life for me. So we call this limitation a disability and try to get rid of it. **The problem is that we can't get rid of it.**

We, as the human race, can't get rid of the limitations we find in our bodies and minds. If we do something about them successfully in one way the limitations appear in another way that is just as bad or worse. For example if someone successfully overcomes arthritis with a powerful anti-inflammation medication he or she will walk further with less pain but will also be subject to serious gastrointestinal and blood complications while also carrying a weighty financial cost. Or if someone enters special education at age 5 they are 95% likely to still be in special education at age 20 as well as isolated, friendless, without prospects of a job or good income and dependent on family or special services. A child who enters the group home system or an institution is far more likely to die at an early age than one in the same physical or mental circumstances who stays with a family. A person labeled mentally ill and sent to therapy of any sort is likely to continue to be labeled no matter what the outcome of the therapy and subject still to stigma and limitation in his or her life.

As if this were not bad enough, there is also no limitation on the world of disability itself. For example I am perfectly eligible to live in a chronic care institution. I have never had the full use of my body in all of my 44 years and taxpayers in Canada would pay $150,000 a year for me to be hospitalized. But 5, 10, even 40 years later I would still have very limited use of my body. People would allow me, even support me, to spend the rest of my life **waiting** to become a person who walks and moves my arms. Worse still, in a shrinking economy where $150,000 becomes a significant outlay of resources the idea will recur: "Why don't we just support people to die with dignity?"

The paradigm of disability loads us down with two insupportable choices. Either we spend endless dollars, time and frustration uselessly attempting to eliminate limitations in each other and getting mad at each other when it doesn't work or we abandon people to attics, isolated special education rooms, group homes, institutions, poor health, wasted lives and even death itself.

Mike: There is a saying that if the only tool you have is a hammer then the whole world looks like a nail. When we fill our thought world with 'disability' we all become effected. If I am a labeled person, a paid helper, a loved one or a community person I am affected by the disability paradigm.

I finally realize in my deepest awareness that my labeled daughter is not disabled. What disabled her possibility was my belief in disability as her parent. What limited her was the professionals around her believing her to be disabled. She is not disabled.

The good news is that a paradigm is only a paradigm after all — and there is another paradigm. That other way of thinking is called 'Giftedness'.

INCLUSION AND GIFTEDNESS

In the Giftedness paradigm all people are gifted.

This thought sounds strange to us because we are used to understanding gifts to be special talents that only a few individuals possess. The usual meaning of 'gifted' is accurate in the Giftedness paradigm — that is that if a person can play classical piano at age 4 or run 26 miles in one day without breathing very hard at the end of it or add a long column of five digit numbers without a calculator — if someone has talents such as these they are gifted.

But in the Giftedness paradigm, 'gifted' has a broader and more ancient meaning. Everyone has gifts — countless ordinary and extraordinary gifts. A gift is anything that one is or has or does that creates an opportunity for a meaningful interaction with at least one other person. Gifts are the fundamental characteristics of our human life and community.

There are two simple gifts that all people have and that every other gift depends on. The first is presence. Since you are here you are embodying the possibility of a meaningful interaction with someone else. If you were not here no one could interact with you. Everywhere that you are is where you are present – there you have the possibility of meaningful interaction.

Secondly you are different from everyone else — in countless ways. Difference is required to make meaning possible. For example just imagine that all human eyes were exactly the same colour. No one would concern themselves with the colour of eyes. But in fact we have brown, blue, green, hazel, black, red and pink eyes. This creates the possibility of songs and poetry about the colour of lovers' eyes, optometrists who sell tinted contact lenses to alter the colours of eyes, plus fashion consultants who match clothing, decor or car interiors to eye colour. — Who knows what other possibilities. Whole careers can arise from eye colour — a very simple difference between individuals.

Meaning is only possible because of difference. This means that human interaction arises from presence and difference. You are different from the next person in hundreds, perhaps thousands, of ways — in your body, your thinking, your experience, your culture, your interests, tastes and desires, your possessions, your relationships, and more. Therefore you are a bundle of hundreds, perhaps thousands, of gifts. So is everyone else.

Community depends on giftedness for its existence. Community arises from past interactions and is created in the present interactions in a dynamic process. For example, wherever you are right now you are likely being supported by a floor. Thirty thousand years ago there were no floors. But along the way people had ideas about buildings, walls, ceilings and floors, about constructing complex structures, about furnishings, about literacy, printing and computers, about paper and ink and books; countless of interactions of countless people over thousands of years in a myriad of different places have led you to be reading a book right now supported without a second thought by a floor.

In the meantime the community continues to be created daily by new interactions. We do countless very simple things everyday like getting up, eating, cleaning ourselves and our places, driving to work, talking on telephones, writing, meeting, counting things, plus many more activities. Meanings — sometimes very complex meanings — are the reasons for each act. Both the existence of places where we act and the acts themselves are expressions of Giftedness — the possibility of meaningful interaction based on differences in how people are, what they do and what they have. Community is both the context and the creation of Giftedness.

Walking is a gift. It offers the possibility of meaningful interaction. Not walking is also a gift — also creating the possibility of meaningful interaction. Speaking is a gift. Not speaking is also a gift. It is a different gift. Seeing and not seeing, hearing and being deaf, behaving in ways people expect and disturbing others, knowing how to put one's trousers on straight and getting one's clothes topsy-turvy are all gifts. They are all different with different potentials but all gifts arising from difference. All gifts add to the mosaic of the potential available to the community.

At first this shift of view point may seem to be merely cosmetic. Perhaps you wonder if I am leaving the door open to calling people 'the differently gifted'. **Not at all! We are all Gifted!**

In fact this shift in paradigm is far more than idealistic or sentimental. Giftedness is strategic and understanding Giftedness is fundamental to achieving full inclusion in community along with active, valued participation and strong networks of relationship.

Mike: People labeled with disabilities and their loved ones are often so conditioned by the disability paradigm that they cannot see gifts or possibilities. It can feel impractical, embarrassing or foolish to have dreams for a 'labeled' loved one who is surrounded by case workers and plans.

> *When people begin to see gifts and begin to participate in the Giftedness paradigm, it is as though a fog has lifted from their eyes. To see gifts after being conditioned to see only deficits and problems is a wrenching, heart opening experience. This different view leads to a new world, it is as simple as a new pair of glasses. We see what we believe.*

The point is that people everywhere understand Giftedness at an intuitive, gut level. People know that Giftedness makes their world 'go round'. They expect to support others in their Giftedness and they expect to have their own Giftedness supported. Supporting Giftedness happens every day, everywhere both in economic and voluntary terms. People of all ages are involved in fulfilling each others' gifts. It is as natural as breathing.

The purpose of this book is to teach you what you already know. You already know how to support Giftedness in other people. You already know how to ask for support for your own Giftedness. When you realize what you already know, you can apply your expert knowledge to support your friend or loved one who has been left out of the community. The community needs them.

Mike: I wrote this poem after two weeks of being in an Inclusive community where gifts and differences were valued. When I first met my daughter after this experience I was struck by how differently I experienced her.

Saturday Morning 7/17/93

I looked into Annie's Eyes this morning—

In this morning I looked in Annie's eyes. My daughter's eyes. I searched for what was wrong. What is her disability? As I looked in her eyes, at her hair blown by night's tossing and turning, she smiled and smiled. My heart hurt with sensations all over. Where is it? I could find no wrong with Annie in her beauty playing with her dog this morning.

Polly danced and barked. Annie sprayed water at Polly's barks. They danced around the room. I felt like I was coming through a thick fog this morning. I cannot see anything wrong with Annie. I cannot feel any where in my body that tight almost nauseous feeling I always have when I think I have seen what's wrong with Annie.

In this morning my body feels no tightness, no nausea as I look, and look at Annie. She is simply a beautiful, joy filled child having morning spraying love and water at her barking dog, Polly.

I sit this morning feeling a trembling in my belly. How precious is this moment of me seeing Annie as she is.

I am angry for all the Labelers who have sought to steal my daughter's life.

I am sad that I have so many times taken their lies inside me seeing Annie as retarded or organic brain damaged or disabled or whatever. I have often seen my child with eyes of guilt and shame. I have been robbed of the present.

It is so obvious at this moment that there are only children.

People filled with gifts and possibilities.

I feel my belly calm, warm, my heart trembling, my eyes with tears, my smile soft. I see Annie so clearly this moment of dog spraying laughter.

I know I do not have to live the Labelers lie. I know in this morning the truth.

SUPPORTS THAT REALLY WORK

Ordinary citizens in community are supported every day to participate and to make a contribution at work, at home, as consumers and in countless other ways. Most of the time, however, they are completely unaware of these support structures. People get to work without thinking about the pavement on the roads, the complex system that puts gas in their cars and donuts in the coffee shop, or the electrical power system that activates the elevator that takes them to their office. If people did have to think about these support structures more than the occasional time when a repair is required their participation and contributions would be seriously hampered.

If we are not going to try to change people and we are not simply going to abandon people to whatever circumstances may befall them, then what can we powerfully change? To find answers to this question, Giftedness sends us looking at meaning, interaction and support structures.

The Giftedness paradigm asks the question: "Where is the limitation, really?" The answer Giftedness gives us is: "The limitation that we **can** change here is in the support structure."

In other words **there are no disabled people**. What is real is that there are people who are vulnerable to being stuck in structures that don't support them, or in interactions that lead to stagnant meaning or deepening isolation. The good news is that meaning, relationships and support structures are all areas where human beings have countless centuries of successful experience in overcoming limitation. Inclusion calls for us to be with vulnerable people using time honoured means of calling forth and supporting contribution.

In this part of the book I will examine what we already know about supporting people to participate.

INVISIBILITY

As we saw in the previous example about work, supports that really work are invisible. This means that the person or people who are being supported to participate are not required to think on a regular basis about the quality, capacity and availability of their supports. They take them for granted and that is as it should be. If these supports were not invisible the person who wants to participate would be using up valuable time and energy making the support structure work.

END USE CHOICE

Although we have relatively little choice on how things work, for example, how the electrical system works or how the roads are built, we do have almost complete choice over how we use ordinary support structures. I decide whether I will buy a car or use a bus and, more importantly, I decide where and when I'm going. I decide when I'm going to turn on a light in my home, what sort of light it will be and what I'm going to use the light for: like cooking or reading. If the lights decided when they were going to come on or the car decided where it was going to go I would have a great deal more difficulty in participating in a way that made sense to me. This means that I would have a great deal of difficulty contributing to my community.

ACCOUNTABILITY

Ordinary support structures demand my accountability in two ways. Firstly I share the cost of the structure. For example, when the snow falls in Toronto publicly paid funded services go into action to clear the streets. However, each citizen who owns property in the city is also required to shovel the sidewalk in front of his or her building. If they don't do this the City Works Department will send someone along to do the shovelling and send the bill directly to the owner. I pay through my taxes and I pay through my actions.

I pay for the cost of a car and its gas or I purchase a bus token. The cost of maintaining the roads is publicly shared. This cost sharing allows for more equity in the use of the support structure while at the same time demanding accountability and therefore responsibility from the users of this support.

Secondly, ordinary support structures demand that I use them in a manner consistent with their original purpose. I may drive a car, but if I drive too fast for other's safety, I will be pulled over. Furthermore, if I were to use the road as a place to lie down and have a nap, I would certainly be picked up and taken elsewhere. As a society we demand that people maintain the integrity of the structure itself. What this means is that we insist that we all have the same meaning for the use of the support structure. The road is for transportation– that is its meaning.

THE NATURE OF NON-PARTICIPATORY SUPPORTS

When we look at support structures which are designed and operated with labeled people in mind we see a completely different picture. First of all specialized support structures are rarely invisible; they demand a very high level of maintenance and attention from their users. For example any parent with a child in special education knows that daily vigilance is required to make sure that transportation doesn't break down, that individual educational goals are being respected and worked towards or even that the child's basic physical requirements such as safety are being addressed.

The fact that specialized supports require such high energy

175

input means that those who depend on them are frequently returning to "square one" when it comes to their level of participation. But the fact that people never get to "square two" is attributed to their label. Labeled individuals get blamed for their relatively low level of competence or contribution.

Secondly, specialized supports are rarely at the control of the person who depends on them. The para-transport bus has a priority towards medical trips and the scheduler usually refuses to take people out for fun. Besides it has to be ordered four days ahead of time even if you want to visit your aunt in the hospital right now. The group home is filled up with people you did not choose to live with and besides it was built in a neighbourhood two hours away from where your supported employment program placed you in a job. This means that you spend four hours a day travelling to do a job you did not choose only to return home to people you do not care about and chores assigned to you by some supervisor.

This lack of choice over how a person will use his or her supports ensures that many possible ways of participating go untapped simply because opportunity to be present is missing. It also means that personal competence will constantly be diminished.

Finally although many public dollars go into establishing and maintaining the specialized support system, cost sharing does not foster responsibility or accountability. For example if I wanted to stay in a chronic care hospital people would pay the cost for me for all of the rest of my life without publicly questioning whether this fostered my making a contribution to society. In turn I would have to pay nothing so long as I agreed to stay dirt poor. In other words first the government would take away all my money and then it would pay all the cost.

Consequently no one in our society is turning to a person with a disability label and saying, "I need what you have to offer. I am willing to support you but I want you to give what you have to give." In this absence of genuine accountability, people are not being called on to be the best they can be.

Furthermore, the specialized support structures have only one meaning at their core. That meaning is, "You are no good until you get fixed." But people with disability labels cannot attach themselves to this meaning. The structure has no integrity for them. They can never be accountable to it. It can never foster their participation. It is just not possible.

I learned about this from one woman in particular. She had been a resident in a group home for many years while one staff person after another came and left. She very much wanted to make this place into a home that was welcoming to everyone. For her, being a homemaker was an important meaning in her life. But to the staff people, the meaning of the group home is a place to take care of her and to supervise her. No one was ever asking her to be accountable for her desire to be a homemaker. Consequently she was always sad, frustrated and lonely. The staff around her were always wondering why she was unhappy and trying to fix her moods. "Group home" can never really mean home.

What is clear is that non-participatory supports create situations in which people experience real barriers to beginning and continuing to contribute to community. Here is where we see the real difference between the disability paradigm and the Giftedness paradigm. In disability resources are expended to overcome limitation, creating much activity but no results in the area of participation. In Giftedness, resources are directed fundamentally in order to foster participation.

RELATIONSHIPS

An important aspect of structures that really support is the network of relationships that exist in people's lives. There are four basic types of relationships that describe the mosaic of people we connect with every day.

Look at the four concentric circles on the next page. (You might actually try this on your own piece of paper.)

In the innermost circle place the names of people with whom you have great intimacy. This is the place for people who are so much a part of your life that it would be difficult to imagine life without them. In fact it does not necessarily have to be people who go in this circle. Some people would place a favorite pet here; others might put a laptop computer. Some people will want to put in the name of someone who has already died.

In the next circle, the second one, put the names of people who are good friends. This the circle of close friendship.

In the third circle put the names of people who you participate with. In this circle also put names of groups and organizations that you typically spend time with and contribute to. So, for example, the third circle can include a group of work colleagues, a tennis club, a church group, the Board of the cooperative grocery store you're part of and two or three individuals you occasionally socialize with.

The fourth circle is the circle of exchange. Put names here of people who you pay to be in your life. Typically people put in the names of a doctor, a dentist, perhaps a hairdresser and often a teacher.

There is an important pattern that emerges for someone who

is participating in the community. In the intimate circle there will be a wide range of possible numbers of people, from 1 to 15 or more. In the circle of close friendship there can be from one or two people to more than 20. In the circle of participation, the third circle, there will rarely be less than 4 and sometimes more than 7. In the exchange circle, the fourth circle, there will rarely be more than 10 people.

The key circle is the third one, the circle of participation. The people who interact at this level are doing so in order to support each other's contributions in that environment. There is a conscious intention to forward the activities agreed on in that situation, whether it be work, tennis or worship. People participating together in the third circle share the same meaning about what they are doing.

Any one individual in this group can count on some level of support from every other individual, because they have a funda-mental agreement that whatever activity is going on is meaning-ful. From this fundamental agreement the beginnings of other relationships and activities are possible. Notice that the people in your second circle usually started out in your third circle. In fact some of the people in your first circle probably started out in your third circle, the circle of participation.

When someone has been labeled into the 'special' world we see a very different pattern emerge in their relationships. There will be a very similar circle of intimacy. In circle two there will usually be fewer people, often none or one or two. In the third circle again there will be usually none or one or two. There will be an explosion in the fourth circle with more than ten, often more than thirty people paid to be in this person's life.

This overburdened fourth circle is a graphic representation

of the gulf between the two paradigms of disability and Giftedness. A person vulnerable to being labeled disabled or excluded on other grounds finds their participation time and energy taken up meeting the demands of interacting with so many people who are paid to 'provide' a service. Each of these people has demands and needs and living with them in your life can be like living perpetually in college at the end of semester when every professor has just one more book for you to read and one more paper for you to write. The demands become overwhelming because you have no opportunity to coordinate priorities, deadlines or objectives.

In the meantime, as the third circle remains barren, the person gains no new relationships, interests or opportunities from which to build a fulfilling circle of close friendship and intimacy. After all circle four relationships are inherently the most unstable since by design they end as soon as the basis of exchange changes. In other words people in circle four are intentionally committed to jobs and money and not to interaction and participation and so any change in funding source or job description can end the relationship.

Once again the person takes on the appearance of incompetence when in fact there is a failure in the support structure. In this case the failure is in the structure of relationships. All people both build and sustain their place in community and a fulfilling network of friends and loved ones from their circle of participation. If this circle is nearly empty and particularly if circle three is being devastated by too many circle four relationships then a person has no foundation for sustaining participation and contribution.

Circle of Support (Friends)
FILL from the OUTSIDE - IN!

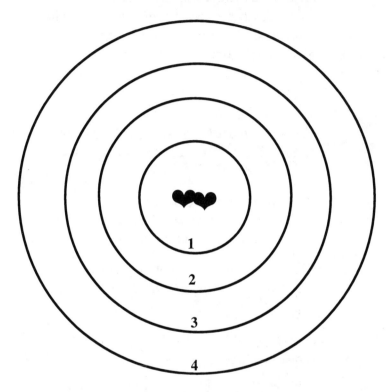

First Circle: *Circle of INTIMACY*
Second Circle: *Circle of FRIENDSHIP*
Third Circle: *Circle of PARTICIPATION*
Fourth Circle: *Circle of EXCHANGE*

Inclusion Press
24 Thome Cres.
Toronto, Ont. Canada M6H 2S5

BASIC PRINCIPLES of ANY STRATEGY for SUPPORTING a PERSON to CONTRIBUTE in COMMUNITY

The above is a basic understanding of how people and relationships work together to create community through gifted interactions. From this, four basic principles emerge for designing any strategy to include someone in the world of participation. They are:

∞ The person must be present.

∞ The person must have sufficient circle three relationships to sustain his or her participation.

∞ The activities must be meaningful both to the person in consideration and those who are part of the place and the activities.

∞ The person must have control over pieces of equipment and money that are critical to the participation he or she is interested in.

Following these principles will open a pathway for anyone to achieve dramatic positive changes in the activities and fulfilment in their life.

Over the years I have come to expect three reactions to the above statement.

The first is: "Great! When can I start." I say: "Go ahead! But don't forget the rest of the book. You might find it helpful."

The second reaction sounds more like: "This can't possibly be this simple. What about all the years that I have struggled?

What about all the people who have said, 'NO'? What about all the `friends' who just quietly left?" I have an answer to this which I know is difficult to absorb all at once.

We have to recognize the power that the disability paradigm has over our minds, our words and our actions. Every person who has ever been labeled disabled, ever loved someone labeled disabled, ever worked to change the lives of vulnerable people or even just heard about or paid for or come close to being involved has become trapped to some extent in the defeating spiral of fixing limitations. When you add to this number all those people who have the same experience but from the point of view of aging or so called `mental health' or `child welfare', etc. it becomes clear that we all experience a barrier to thinking and acting with integrity when it comes to creating community with people we find to be different. I will come back to this in a final chapter.

Meanwhile the third reaction I have come to expect is: "How do you determine what the meaning of an activity will be? Particularly how do you do this if the person in question doesn't speak or communicate clearly? How do you find people who will find this person's participation meaningful?"

In order to answer these important questions over the years I have asked many people where the meaning of their lives came from. In particular I carefully watched the unfolding of the lives of several people who do not speak. I questioned their loved ones and caregivers about how they knew what would make sense and why some people seemed to accomplish far more than others when faced with similar barriers and circumstances. I want to share my discoveries about Dreaming and Listening.

DREAMING AND LISTENING

Everybody dreams. By dreaming I mean the process that leads you and I to be sitting almost unconscious, perhaps staring out a window not seeing, imagining ourselves to be doing something or experiencing something.

Most of the time we don't think about our dreams. We imagine that our fantasies or reveries are of no importance. But fantasy is only one form of dreaming. It is the form that has the least impact on the community – the most private form.

Dreaming itself has no words. Our fantasies are expressions of our dreams. Many of the expressions of our dreams are more public and political. Dreaming is the beginning and the context of relationship and of all our creativity.

We can never fully know our dreams since they exist in a realm that has no language. Every expression that we make of our dreams captures only a likeness of them. But it is also true that since language is not essential to dreaming those who do not speak or who communicate in ways that seem unusual, incomplete or 'off-base' are dreaming right along with everyone else.

I used to have a very compelling fantasy about being a truck driver. I would sit for long minutes imagining that I was behind the wheel of a sleek 18-wheeler driving some important delivery to California, which is more than 4000 miles from where I live. I would imagine earning enough money driving my rig that I would have to work only six months of the year. The other six months I would put my feet up, so to speak, comfortably at home.

Now it is very unlikely that I will ever drive any truck. I have very limited use of my limbs since I have essentially no power in most of my motor muscles. So not only would I spend time in this

184

fantasy but for many years I also spent time feeling guilty about this pursuit. But finally my interest in discovering the nature of meaning caused me to examine in a non-judgemental way my own experience.

I discovered over time that my fantasy represented the dream that I have a life where my work would be the focus. In other words the life of a workaholic was, and still is, meaningful to me. Beyond this the fantasy was telling me that a high degree of travel and mobility are satisfying to me. It's also important that I be bringing something of value to other people. Years after I began to examine this story I discovered another level of meaning. I discovered that the time spent at work needed to be balanced with restful and reflective time at home.

Nowadays I never spend time fantasizing about truck driving. I'm too busy travelling internationally to deliver the message of Giftedness and Inclusion. Over the years my support circle and I have learned to ask for enough money from my workshops so that I can afford a restful home in Toronto where I can prepare for the physical demands of travel and gather stories, reflections and insights about community. This part of my dream is very much part of the public domain and I am fulfilled.

It took many years to reach the point in my life where the truck driver version of my dream no longer was necessary to point the way toward where meaning lay in my life. The process of listening to one's own dream and those of others is no instant solution to an annoying problem but a doorway to a room to be revisited over and over again. Nevertheless even short visits to the world of dreams can give us strong clues as to where meaningful opportunity lies in someone's life.

Dream is at the heart of all human creativity. All that we take for granted and depend upon in life did not exist at some point in our human history. Over the centuries people shared their ideas and experience about tools and buildings, about ways of getting around, about ways of organizing ourselves and being together, and so much more. They shared these ideas and experience out of a large variety of dreams about what would make things better or make sense or just plain be good to have around.

Through this process – of working together on the basis of shared dreams – reality as we experience it daily is created. In turn daily reality shapes the way we express our inexpressible dream in words and ideas.

A woman that I met several years ago gave me a story which explains this dynamic process. I met her in her early fifties. She told me that when she was a teenager she had dreams of being a missionary. But war years and other circumstances intervened and she got married, then had several children. Sometimes it seemed to her that her dream of being a missionary had died yet other times it re-emerged. As a sort of gesture to this dream she would occasionally join a Bible class or go on a weekend Christian retreat. Then her marriage began to break down. She discovered a fledgling form of family support, called Marriage Encounter, born in the Episcopalian tradition. She dragged her unwilling husband into it. Shortly thereafter he became an enthusiastic participant. Not only was their marriage bolstered but both she and her husband went on to become international leaders in the Marriage Encounter movement. A few years later she could tell me that Marriage Encounter had become the fulfilment of her dream.

Another way of looking at this process is that her dream

never was really about being a missionary. As a teenager, being a missionary was the closest experience she had encountered at that time to express her dream. If she had actually become a missionary she might have found after some time that there were major parts of her dream still unfulfilled. As it was, her dream kept her motivated to continue to try various experiences in her own religious tradition. So reality shaped the expression of her dream.

As she and her husband took on leadership roles, their shared expression of their dreams shaped reality. Without people like herself and her husband adding their energy and creativity, an invention like Marriage Encounter dies away as just another short lived fad. In this way we can see that daily reality emerges from dreaming – in turn daily reality shapes the expression of dream.

The strength and vitality of community depends on how many people are getting a chance to have their dreams expressed in daily reality. Understanding the nature of dream faces us with questions of ethics.

First of all not every expression of a dream has the same value in the community. For example I have a dream that no children will ever again go to bed hungry. One expression of my dream could be for me to raise up a gang of thieves who go about stealing food to give to hungry children. Another expression would be to become a political lobbyist who tries to bring in a guaranteed annual income to all people. A third would be to try to make sure there were no children. Each is a valid expression of my dream but each has very different consequences for me, for children and for the community in general.

Secondly, community will be enriched if everyone has approximately equal support to be at work bringing their dreams into daily reality. Yet throughout all of history some people have had much more support than others to fully express their dreams. Furthermore these people rarely are subject to the scrutiny of the community to determine if the particular expression of their dream has good consequences for the community at large. So for example if the president of a multinational corporation decides that he must move a car manufacturing company from one country to another there is little to be done about it even though hundreds of lives will be disrupted.

Other cultures have handled the ethics of dreaming differently. In an Amish community people have decided to use the internal combustion engine for farming but not for transportation based on their perception of the likely consequences for the community. They have concluded that moving too fast disrupts relationship.

In order to preserve their families and friendships, they have decided not to go any faster than a horse can carry them. Communities clogged by cars, smog and stress might do well to listen.

Inclusion holds as fundamental that all people are dreamers. Inclusion assumes that community is stronger when all dreams are brought into the political process of creating reality. It also assumes that the expressions of our dreams must be open to scrutiny to determine that the unfolding consequences will not weaken the community. Inclusion is a holistic belief system with its own integrity.

Mike: People who are labeled or their loved ones are not allowed to believe dreams are possible for them. They are led to believe in the disability paradigm — that their need is for case plans, assessments and interventions rather than for hopes, creation and dreams. Then people wonder why their plans fail?

Since dreaming is at the heart of relationship, Giftedness, creation, meaning, interactions, community and therefore Inclusion we are compelled to become listeners of dreams. Fortunately the task is an energizing one.

I learned much about listening from a friend who uses no words and who recently, in his 25th year, has begun to use facilitated communication. Throughout the span of his teenage years he was a caterer, a courier, an office assistant, a sound poet, a neighbourhood organizer and an evangelist. He accomplished all this because his family surrounded themselves with a circle of people whose commitment was to listen for the family's dreams and to help them find the resources they needed to make these dreams part of the community.

At age 14 their son was faced with being segregated in a classroom set up for people labeled 'severely mentally retarded'. When they realized the devastating effect this segregation was having on him they decided to put his dream of having friends his own age and lots of interesting things to be part of into action. They used family money to hire a daily companion.

The breakthrough was that this companion had a job description that conforms with Giftedness and community. He was hired with the intention of finding places where my friend would find interesting activities and people who enjoyed his participation. The companion listened with his actions, with his questions and with an open mind. For three months the pair travelled together to all parts of the city checking out schools, community organizations, coffee shops and other nooks and crannies. Once in a welcoming school the companion followed up on interests and initiatives from the other students. He supported them to try new activities with my friend and to keep on interacting on the basis of interest, curiosity, insight, or whatever each new day brought.

As the years unfolded the companion used each new learning about the growing boy and about the people around to try new places and new activities. The results were phenomenal in the range and number of both friends and projects that emerged. My friend was more involved as a teenager than are most 'typical' people.

Dreams can only perform their work of creating the world when people listen to each other's dreams. By ourselves we can only express our dreams as fantasies. **The process of creating action with results involves first of all listening to a dream, then reaching agreement on the value of the dream to the listeners, finding a mutually acceptable concrete expression**

of the dream and finally planning and sharing action.

In a society such as ours there is no agreement that everyone will have people to listen to their dreams. But this does not have to be a barrier to those who want to bring Inclusion to the world. With a commitment to dream and to listen to others' dreams and to find listeners for the dreams of those we care about — with these commitments we can bring about dramatic changes and improvements in the lives of people who would otherwise remain isolated from the creative activity of community.

What is listening? It is doing whatever it takes to be able to imagine yourself living with the same experiences, concerns and interests as the person you are listening to. Real listening can mean anything from sitting and listening with your ears to walking down a street with someone to discover what captures their interest. We can all do it and with practice and commitment we can learn to listen at a level which can energize ourselves and the person we are listening to. Listening to a person causes that person to be able to know their own dream better than before and to know what the next step in bringing that dream about could be.

In other words, **even if all we can do is listen, this is the most important step in supporting someone toward bringing their dream into daily community.** To listen is to be a mirror in which another person can see themselves in a new way. Along with the new vision comes a new sense of what steps are possible and a new energy from connecting to the dream itself.

Any strategy that is to be designed to bring someone into active life in the community must have both a foundation in and an ongoing way to listen to the person's dream. Without this process being fully honoured the strategy is doomed to being fruitless busy work.

DESIGNING SUPPORTS THAT WORK TO SUSTAIN PARTICIPATION IN THE COMMUNITY

The four basic principles of designing a strategy that works are:

- ∞ The person must be present.

- ∞ The person must have sufficient circle three relationships to sustain his or her participation.

- ∞ The activities must be meaningful both to the person in consideration and those who are part of the place and the activities.

- ∞ The person must have control over pieces of equipment and money that are critical to the participation he or she is interested in.

When these strategies are woven together within an Giftedness framework great things are possible.

This participation will be valued by the community of participants. They will tolerate and often even welcome a large range of diversity. In other words what in the disability paradigm is a problem to be fixed becomes of no consequence or even of positive advantage when people are working in the Giftedness paradigm.

PRESENCE

It may seem obvious that a person must be present in the community before they can become participants in the community, but nevertheless it is amazing how often presence is not taken into consideration. For example, a school may go to a great deal of effort to establish a network of friendships around a child who has become isolated only to have these efforts continually frustrated. Upon examination of the actual activities of the children it can be seen that the children carry out most of their meaningful interactions in the half hour before class starts and the hour after class finishes as well as during brief and informal times in the bathrooms, etc. But the isolated child arrives on a 'special ' transportation vehicle 15 minutes after class has started and leaves 1 half hour before class ends. Furthermore, while other children are interacting informally, this child is being 'served' by an adult caregiver in a different location. Even heroic efforts at integration will fail since the child is never truly present in the community.

Presence as a fundamental condition of Inclusion is ignored in other ways. For example, advocates will sometimes work many years to change policies and guidelines while the people they are concerned about continue to live and work in segregation. In many cases this means that advocates waste years of effort since the actual change in policy can have no effect on the lives of the segregated people.

On the other hand when presence is paid attention to much can be accomplished in an environment that is still otherwise devoted to disability. For example my friend's companion was hired to take my friend and go look for places where his presence would be appreciated. Over the years they found dozens of such places.

Mike: People need to be present in ordinary community and use ordinary, general resources as much as possible. People 'labeled' are usually 'serviced' by many extraordinary, segregated services. For example my child is encouraged to use the services of an Occupational Therapist rather than offered support to go to dance lessons.

RELATIONSHIPS

People can be present and still very isolated. Much of the work of bringing somebody into community and sustaining their participation involves creating and maintaining circle three relationships.

Some people find this aspect challenging because they consider relationships of participation to be 'natural' -- i.e. unstructured. In fact we direct much of the public resources of our society toward sustaining circle three life. The people that we care about have mainly been left out or pushed out and we must devise ways to have these relationships take hold.

The essential binding of circle three relationships is meaning - the participants understand the meaning and value that the participation they share in common has for each other. Given that meaning is driven by dream I will write about these principles together.

MEANINGFULNESS

The heart of all strategies that work is meaningful participation. Both the individual who is becoming part of the community and those who will share the circle three must find meaning in their interaction. Most strategies that fail do so because of a mismatch in this area. For example if someone says: "I know a mentally retarded person who wants to join your fishing club.", don't be surprised if the person is refused. On the other hand if someone says: "I know someone who loves fish stories who wants to join your fishing club.", then that person has opened up an entirely different possibility.

Where to look for meanings that will bind people together is in dreams; both the dreams of the person who is to be included and the people who are at least potentially part of circle three. In the situation of the fishing club one does not have to look too far since anglers dream of fish and all that goes along with fishing. Meaningful participation could be established around watching a Saturday afternoon fish show on TV.

In other situations a deeper look may be required. In the case of my friend, his companion began his work around my friend's obvious interest in food. Most of the initial visits were to coffee and donut shops, grocery stores to perform odd jobs and to neighbours for a friendly cup of tea. In time this led to my friend having an important position at school helping to prepare lunches. Even later he became very close to a priest that he met at a Thursday lunch gathering. Food was not only the beginning of the process but it turned out to be the thread that wove through six years of activities.

Mike: Inclusion suggests a way of being in the world where
differences are gifts. So often in our world people

> *have been taught to fear what is different. In the*
> *disability paradigm differences lead to threats or*
> *rewards, where as in the Giftedness model differences*
> *are an invitation to novelty, creativity and the*
> *excitement of contact with other human beings.*
> *Holding the difference opens the door to living.*

Very often the initial expressions of a person's dream will seem very unrealistic. This is OK – all expressions of our dreams are essentially unrealistic. Reality is created out of dream. When a person expresses his or her dream as a fantasy, it only means they have very little experience. Listeners can hear the meaning of this dream anyway.

For example, someone may say that they want to become a doctor when it is quite clear that they do not have the interests or skills to become involved in long academic studies. In the disability paradigm people would tell that person to give up that dream since it is unrealistic. In the Giftedness paradigm we can ask: "What would becoming a doctor mean to you? What have you seen doctors do that you would like to be involved in? What is the first step for you to become a doctor?" In one such situation the person responded by saying that his first step would be to get a volunteer job in a hospital. In a very short period of time he was gainfully employed helping to package sterile supplies. He became proud and happy and people respected and depended on his contribution. He gained a small number of lunch buddies. His dream was fulfilled.

Circle three relationships can be formed and sustained by the act of listening to dreaming, especially if opportunities for listening are created on a frequent basis. This is particularly true in the situation where a support circle is part of the sustaining strategy. I will say more about this shortly.

Circle three relationships will break down if other participants have not been engaged in the process of coming to understand how this activity is meaningful to this person. For example if a child who has no interest in academics is present in a regular classroom but none of the children or their parents understand in what way this participation is meaningful to this person, there is certain to be a breakdown. One of the places where this breakdown will happen will be in the level of informal supports offered to this person. For example fellow classmates will fail to make a Valentine's Day card for this child even though every other child gets one.

This sort of breakdown is easy to prevent or repair. Make sure that everyone in the place of participation has had a chance to talk about why this person is there. Make sure they can get all of their questions answered. Make sure that they can say for themselves what the meaning of this person's participation is. It may require a formal meeting, but often it only requires some informal chat. Once the understanding of the meaning of this persons participation is there, people will "naturally" offer their support.

CONTROL OVER EQUIPMENT AND MONEY

Circle three relationships will break down if the person is not actually able to participate in the way anticipated.

In order to prevent this sort of breakdown insure that the person has control over pieces of equipment and money that are important to make their participation happen. The critical resources can also be determined by listening to the person's unfolding dream.

For example, my truck driver fantasy told me that I should have control over my truck. Now in my more real expression of this dream the meaning is that I have to have control over my mobility. This means for me that I need a fairly complex set of supports that involves a motorized wheelchair that I can drive with my thumb, a van equipped with a wheelchair lift, a range of personal assistants all of whom can drive and a way of sitting in an airplane seat that supports my body. Another individual might have very similar physical functioning to me but a dream that called for control over different things. For example such a person might be quite happy to get around town on the para-transport bus but want to have control over environmental aspects of her apartment such as light switches, thermostats, etc.

When an individual has important equipment and money at their disposal they can function with the same level of informal supports that other circle three participants expect and offer. For example my friend had his companion to go to school with, and his companion would provide guidance on the bus, personal assistance with physical needs, etc. With this support, my friend participated like every other student at that school in the informal meetings where students thought up and designed new courses to put on in their high school. It was at one of these gatherings that the students noticed how my friend makes many unusual noises, and his companion supported them in their curiosity, again acting as an important support. The students designed a class on sound poetry and my friend became just one of several performers at a sound poetry evening. As they became more familiar to each other the students became willing to fill in for the companion if he was going to be unavailable. But if they had been forced to provide this level of support in the beginning stages it is quite possible that my friend's participation would have been rejected.

This area of control over critical equipment and money is one that advocates must take a close look at. There are many possible goals to advocate for, and an advocate – especially one who is also a relative and a caregiver – can easily become exhausted in their relationship with the person they are working with. It is important to choose one's battles carefully in order not to suffer a breakdown in relationship. Fighting for control over critical pieces of equipment and money is important since success will help sustain renewed participation and thus bring new energy to the advocate's relationship with the participant.

BUILDING SUPPORT CIRCLES

A support circle is a circle three phenomenon. It has a specific intention of gathering to listen to a person's dream and creating the resources and openings required to bring this person's dream into the community. Its focus remains on the person who is vulnerable to being isolated and being a non-participant. In spite of this focus all the members of the circle typically will experience their participation in the circle as a vehicle for examining and improving their own contributions to society.

Although a support circle is not always necessary it has a unique power for rapidly changing the life experience of an individual who experiences great barriers to participation. A support circle has the power of being an invention in the area of relationship, meaning and interaction and so has access to all the formal and informal supports that are 'natural'.

The following are the steps required to create a support circle:

1) Find a circle facilitator.

This person's job description includes:

    a) Helping to figure out who the circle is for.

    b) Helping with the initial invitation.

    c) Keeping the circle meeting.

    d) Making sure that the focus person says 'Yes' to something that the circle offers.

Many of the complications of building a circle are indicated in this job description.

(a) [Who Circle is for] First of all it can often be a little mind-bending figuring out who the circle is for in the beginning. In the situation where the focus person is an adult who speaks for themselves the scenario is fairly straight forward but such situations are rare it seems to me. It is much more typical to be involved in situations where one person is the named focus but the real focus is on a parent or an advocate who typically speaks for this person. There is nothing wrong with a parent or an advocate being the focus – in fact when the circle involves children it is basically essential that the circle be formed around the parent(s). The issue is simply that when the focus is confused the process gets unclear and the action stalls. Therefore it is essential that this issue be sorted out, likely on many different occasions.

Occasionally the focus of the circle will shift for a short period of time. This is a good thing unless for some reason it is difficult to return the focus to the person the circle started for. In such a situation consider starting two circles that are interconnected by having some joint membership. This is a useful strategy in situations like a teacher with a vulnerable child in a regular classroom or a parent with a teenager who is vulnerable to being labeled. For example the teacher could have a circle of adults including the parents of the child and some of the child's classmates and the child could have a circle of children from the class and from the neighbourhood.

(b) [Initial Invitation] Helping with the inviting is a critical stage often full of struggle. People typically say that they do not know anyone. This is absolutely not true yet in a certain sense the experience is quite real. After all it is to be expected that the person's life is full of circle four people plus lots of other people who have been carefully trained by society to see this individual as limited and in need of fixing. The dynamics of the disability paradigm make it almost a dead certainty that all these people have been interacting in ways that push each other away. It doesn't occur to the individual in question that some of these very same people are able to and in fact would love to move from circle four to circle three or from other aspects of circle three, two or one into a circle three support circle.

(c) [Keeping Circle Meeting] The job of keeping the circle meeting arises because circles typically experience either great success or unexpected overwhelming barriers right at the beginning. In either situation the disability paradigm teaches us to give up because if we have succeeded then the situation must be fixed and if we have failed it must be unfixable. It usually takes time for people to catch the flavour of Inclusion and Giftedness. **In fact the person is included as soon as the circle begins to meet.** It is the journey of interactions and meanings and the listening to dreams that counts much more than the outward successes. In time, as the circle experiences Inclusion and as 'successes' emerge from unexpected directions, the issue of meeting will be less critical.

The point is that the support circle is the vehicle of listening to dream and the listening must continue until there are enough other possibilities of listening in the individual's circle three. Even then, life is very fragile, and the circle may need to come together if the ghost of 'disability' raises its head again.

(d) [Getting to Yes] Perhaps the biggest surprise will be in how much work there is in getting someone to say 'Yes'. In many subtle and devious ways people have learned to say 'No'. When a circle listens to a dream the listeners will begin to offer all sorts of opportunities and resources to the focus person. They do this because they are human and not because anyone asks them to. People will make suggestions of other people that might like to join the circle; they will offer to find jobs; they will offer to come and help out; they will offer to go to meetings or write letters; they will offer to make cookies; etc., etc.

And the focus person will say 'No' to it all. They will say 'No' because it is the wrong people; They will say 'No' because it's the wrong job; they will say 'No' because they can do it better themselves; they will say 'No' because they don't like cookies; etc., etc. This is all disability paradigm behaviour again. People don't realize that No limits possibility and that Giftedness can only grow out of Yes. In the world of Inclusion the decision to say 'No' must be taken only after careful reflection and because there is a boundary to possibility that you want to make. It is the facilitator's job to get people to say 'Yes'.

It is a rare person that can be his or her own facilitator. It is just too easy to get caught up in the traps that the disability paradigm has laid out for us over the centuries. The most important step you may ever take for yourself is to ask someone you trust to be your support circle facilitator.

2) Invite

The focus person and the facilitator sit down and make a list of 20 - 40 people that the person knows and trusts enough to invite into his or home, (in the absence of a home some comfortable, informal space). The invitation is to listen to the focus person's dream. Make sure that people understand that they are welcome to offer suggestions and resources but that there is no necessity of this. The gift they are being asked to bring is their listening.

3) Dreaming

Some people dream by telling their story and then talking about their hopes and fears. Some talk about fantasies or an ideal day. Some invite others in the group to share dreams as well. Some use photos, drawings, flipcharts or graphs. Some ask a favoured friend to speak for them. Some serve tea and cookies first. Do whatever it takes to get the focused person's dream articulated and to start the listening.

4) Keep meeting; keep saying 'Yes'

The process of meeting, listening, saying 'Yes', experiencing the results, meeting, listening, saying 'Yes', and so on opens up new possibilities, changes the person's expression of his or her dream and brings new people both into the interaction and often into the circle. Over time membership in the circle will change significantly while at the same time a small stable core group develops. At this time I have 5 or 6 individuals who nearly always will be present at my once or twice a year formal meeting. I see these individuals in other contexts in my life almost daily. We invite dozens of people to the formal meetings and this cast of characters changes every time.

The person's expression of his or her dream may change dramatically and rapidly in the first few months or years of having a listening support circle. Experience promotes this change – so does being listened to. A new circle may feel like they are on a roller coaster ride, perhaps even blaming the focus person for some kind of inconstancy. The facilitator's job of keeping the meetings going and of getting people to 'Yes' is very important at this time.

5) Getting back on track

As in all of life it is inevitable that a support circle will get off track. That is to say that the circle will lose its focus on the dream of the focus person and get mired in 'fixing' activity, or get into a pattern of long discussions about trivia, or turn every meeting into a party, etc. When this happens the focus person will likely do one of two things; get sick or behave in aggressive and hostile ways.

At this juncture the facilitator must simply get everyone together and do some serious dreaming and listening. Like all life the creation of participation has its ebbs and flows. A crisis can contain the seeds of a new fruitful beginning if people are supported to listen for new possibility.

Mike: I am facilitating a circle of support with a woman that I used to do family therapy with. I used to see her as a good hearted woman, dependant on therapists, myself included, who was troubled, fearful and unable to parent her children effectively.

I now am the facilitator of her circle of support. I am becoming her friend. We call each other at home. I still offer her any therapy-type assistance but only if she requests it. She is saying 'Yes' to life in many ways within the strength of her circle.

I cannot believe how different she looks to me today from when I was her therapist. Is she that different? No. She is growing and she is struggling still as well. The big difference is that I am now able to see her as a whole person within the context of her worthwhile community rather than a troubled person needing to be surrounded by services. She is happier and, also important, so am I. We both enjoy our work and our friendship very much!

CIRCLE THREE SUPPORT FROM CIRCLE FOUR

The world of circle four can be a powerful inhibitor of participation and contribution. The commitments and intentions of exchange-based relationships foster sustaining production, plans and projects, etc. and work against more informal relationships.

More importantly the disability paradigm is a powerful stimulant to circle four as so much money can exchange hands in the name of fixing someone. As John McKnight (see introduction) often has graphically pointed out circle four has the power to devastate community through convincing people that some expert somewhere has the knowledge and experience to know better than ourselves what will make our lives work. Then imagining that we can 'be better', we give up our dreams for the ones that the 'expert' would sell to us and the management that will define our lives.

As powerfully true as this is there is still a role for paid people in the lives of people vulnerable to exclusion. For example my body is liberated by a team of personal assistants who, in various shifts throughout the day, do the driving, pushing, lifting, physical support, housekeeping, listening, etc. that allows me to move through my busy day accomplishing what there is to do. Like a gang of roadies they keep my show on the road. My personal assistants and my friend's companion are examples of a type of paid support that is often essential to a good strategy for creating participation.

Bluntly put, what makes this support work is that I am the boss. My support circle and I worked for years and continue to remain vigilant to ensure that the money that goes for my assistants' salaries is directed by me. I decide who gets what because I have the control over the money. We make very sure the government sees it this way. In years when there wasn't enough government funding we raised money for salaries to keep a stable team around me.

My friend's family used their own money. They put their son and his circle in the driver's seat. Salary money is often a critical resource that people need control over.

The other factor that makes this important circle four support effective is control over the job description. My personal assistant and my friend's companion have job descriptions that only emphasize participation, not fixing.

Is there never a role for the expert fixer? Sometimes a person's dream directs them to do therapy of some kind. For example my breathing is very vulnerable since I only have a very tiny set of lungs and not too many muscles to move them with. My dream tells me to be constantly on the look out for better exercises and ventilators that will support my continued breathing. My circle knows my doctors and they know my circle. My circle helps me decide how to express my dream consistently with good breathing.

When therapy is consistent with a person's dream and under the control of circle three it can be fruitful. It becomes not much more significant than going to the gym three times a week for aerobics.

Service Brokerage is an example of a circle four service format which can be under the control of circle three. In Service Brokerage a family, individual or circle can hire a skilled broker:

- familiar with dream based planning;

208

• skilled at finding supportive community environments;

• adept at establishing interaction and relationships;

• good at building and sustaining support circles and other circle three networks.

Service Brokerage can be very powerful when the money to hire a broker is under the control of the family, individual or circle, if the broker is truly skilled and if the individual has control over critical resources. But as in all 'special' human services, without these factors in place and safeguarded circle four can easily eliminate participation.

Perhaps this is a good time for a last word on advocacy. Advocates are easily co-opted into behaving as circle four 'volunteers', sitting on committees, setting up 'better' services, writing policy, etc. In the meantime the relationship that brought them into the work in the first place often becomes quite strained and their own place in circle three becomes tenuous. If advocacy is a true expression of a person's dream then it can be fruitful. Otherwise it can easily be a circle four trap.

HUMAN SUPPORT RATHER THAN HUMAN SERVICE
- THE MAKING OF A REVOLUTION

The Giftedness paradigm presents a genuine challenge to anyone who has built their life from being a circle four professional in human services. There is no denying that creating opportunities for people to participate in community can only be successful if people make efforts to forswear, quite literally put up a boundary to resist, the disability paradigm. We must live like an alcoholic determined not to drink in a culture that speaks daily to us of limitations, limitations, limitations. Those determined to build community have to become ever better at making a personal commitment to living from Giftedness, at avoiding environments and processes that speak disability and at surrounding oneself with every sort of relationship that will foster awareness of the ways of Inclusion.

Mike: Inclusion is a spiritual practice. It is a practice of the heart. You have to do it to get it. I am realizing more and more that Inclusion is not primarily something learned through the mind but something discovered through intentionally putting oneself in structures that foster the experience of valuing differences.

The person who is paid to provide service can make a real and lasting contribution to the lives of people vulnerable to exclusion. It is not a question of running from circle four; it is our culture which is the source of the disability paradigm. Every person equally is faced with the challenge of adopting disability as a working philosophy or of working to bolster liberation through Giftedness. The paid professional worker is going to face the extra challenge of working against his or her own self interest by having to resist the general thinking, structures and rewards of the 'special' human service system.

What works for a professional worker is what works in general. Give up disability, its language and its forms. Practice Inclusion to learn Inclusion. Dream. Invite people to listen to your dream. Say 'Yes'. Listen to other people's dreams. Listen. Give up doing what doesn't work. Invite diversity into your own life. Recruit a coach (facilitator). Listen!

The opportunity is here to fulfil the dream that brought you into human service in the first place. The opportunity is here to practice the best of all it can mean to be human. The opportunity is here to actually make a difference in the lives of some people. The opportunity is here to renew our culture and the world.

Mike: Helpers who want to assist another person must begin with that person's expressed dream. Speaking the dream is the beginning of all support.

If the focus person has not expressed their dream nothing will happen. There must be a tenacious commitment to listen and assist as the person expresses his or her dream — draw it, speak it, sound it, walk it. It must be expressed and it must be heard.

Labeled people are seldom listened to. They have a tremendous struggle to be heard. I am beginning to realize how much of the human service system is about trying to get people to agree to follow our ideas of what they should do, ought to do or would be better off to do.

I have put so much effort into trying to know

what 'I' can do to help people. Now I am putting that much effort into trying to know what people I work for really want and dream about, what they want to work on and what they are ready to do.

LOVE WILL GROW

Mike: I have stayed at Judith's home this week as we have worked on this writing about what's really worth doing.

Judith's home is in a cooperative apartment building which intentionally includes people, encourages valuing diversity and whose members commit to 'neighbourliness' in welcoming and supporting one another. Some 44 adults, several dogs, cats, children, a variety of support persons and constant visitors create this lively community.

The feel of the cooperative is striking in comparison to typical apartment buildings or neighbourhoods. I have thought a great deal about how to describe the effect of the coop community upon me.

First, I realize that what Judith and her closest circle of friends speak about all over at workshops and conferences is truly present in the moment to moment life of the coop. The words become real here.

All my adult life I have yearned for what I knew at times as a child and at moments as an adult. I've wanted to be surrounded by loving friends like a moveable kids party, college dorm or best friends baseball game in the summer evening. I finally reached the point where I abandoned this possibility of real community. I sadly concluded my adult life would never hold the ongoing intensively rich closeness of youth where nothing in the world was more important than friend's love.

The coop is very much an expression of what I always dreamed about—a living community. People stand, roll, sit in the hallways talking, gesturing, laughing together any time of day or evening. Judith's front door is usually propped open as we write at the computer. People keep popping in with news of the weather, (it's very cold), community meetings, dogs to walk, who is coming to morning coffee, jokes and laughs, hugs and cookies. The boundaries between people's private living space and others is clear yet permeable. There is an obvious commitment to inviting one another to participate. People get the wonderful healing experience of hearing 'Yes' a lot. "Yes do come in, do join me, let's do it together, yes we can." I am so aware of the energy in the air from this climate where people feel such encouragement to risk being who they really are.

This community is a structure for people to experience each other as gifts. The constant valuing of diversity and intention to experience difference as opportunity is very unusual. I was at a dinner party last evening where one guest used facilitated communication to speak. I was touched by how the effort in our group was not towards fitting him into us but rather people were taking responsibility to carefully listen to his communication. Our struggle was to hear him, rather than struggling to make him a 'better' communicator. When we could hear him he communicated very powerful ideas.

I left this evening realizing how differences not valued cost us so much. When I don't hear another's struggle to communicate, or can't experience another's way of being in the world, I deprive myself of their gifts to me and, in a sense, cheat myself of seeing myself as whole and loving. When people are vulnerable and real with me I am easily invited to forgive my vulnerable feelings and really be me.

As I leave today to fly back to Colorado, I am clear about what the coop is at the centre. Finally, the Inclusive cooperative where Judith lives is an act of love. What we all really need to do is create structures, moments, circles, relationships where love will grow. In places where people with labels, family loved ones, support people and typical community neighbours commit to really be with each other, love will grow.

IN CONCLUSION - DANCING

It is always a little hard for me to know to say good-bye. I have a tendency to just stop dead in a speech or to leave a room when a gathering is concluding. So for awhile I thought I might just stop this book.

Then I thought of completing the circle. Here am I, surrounded by the home I love best, the Courtyard Cooperative; and by those who, like Mike, helped birth this writing; and by those who, like Kerrie and Miriam, have fed me in the last few days, brought the daily news of goings-on in the coop and come to put hands over my eyes to remind me that there is more to life than a computer screen. I am loved and I have ample opportunity to return and acknowledge love.

In the great mystery of life how did I get to be so fortunate? More to the point how can I fully respond to this great gift of life and love?

I can only say that I believe that it is my greatest responsibility and also my greatest joy to try to point to the way — the way out of disability and into life and love. This way is called Inclusion. It is the embracing and honouring of difference. It is the discovery and practice of Giftedness.

I am adding a note that Mike sent to me some weeks afterwe finished the first draft. To me it is an affirmation that Giftedness and Inclusion are truly a pathway to liberation.

Mike: I realize a sense of security about Annie in the world which is new for me. I am perhaps beginning to realize that there is possibility for her to thrive in the world even when I am gone. I watched her get on her bus this morning and felt a peace at her presence, at my backing off at some level, and at my realizing deeply that her security like mine is ultimately in her relations, her people. If she has community, she has life. Somehow a quality of anxious attachment to Annie is shifting. Her well being is between God, Annie and her circle through life.

What is really worth doing is dancing with all the rich possibility that life offers. Enjoy the dance!

Annie At Sweet Sixteen at her PS-1 School

by Mike Green
(an update to 1998)

Annie always says, " I am sweet sixteen." She will be sweet seventeen soon. The last five years since Judith's book was published have been good for Annie.

Our whole family has been very active in developing a new small public school in Denver called PS-1. This school community is the center of Annie's world. She has become a valuable part of the school community. Annie knows for the first time in her life, outside her family, that she is really needed. She has always been in inclusive settings but has seldom experienced herself as a valuable contributor.

One story reminds me of this shift from "Annie who needs us" to Annie "whom we need" is when she was in a choir at PS-1 two years ago. The teacher telephoned us at home one day to find out why Annie was not at choir. I told her Annie was sick with the flu. The teacher said, "We need Annie. She has an important part." I was thinking out loud, "They need her. What can we do about this?" Then I heard a voice from Annie's bedroom, "They need me; they need me!" As sick as she was, Annie wanted to go to school and the choir practice immediately. We talked, and then I took her. The flu didn't matter nearly as much as belonging. Nothing was more important than Annie knowing she was really needed.

This school did not have a philosophy about including people with disabilities. There were no special educators involved in the beginning. What was central was the commitment that all

218

kids were to be taken seriously, listened to, and helped to develop their gifts. Annie was just one of those kids who happened to be slower thinking than average. Her label never has defined her place in the school. The school's founder, Rex Brown, says, "All kids are poets. Our job is to help them find their poetry." Kids, teachers, other parents have always been part of a circle of support for Annie's participation in the PS-1 community. It is definitely not the special education people alone.

When I think about why our school has worked so well for Annie I think of three things. First, it is a real community. PS-1 started with sixty families. It has grown to over 200 families. We think our most serious challenge is how to stay small as we get bigger. Most schools are institutions rather than communities. If schools are not communities for students without disabilities, how on earth can they be places to develop community for students with disabilities? What is most important for Annie is that it has been a real community with real relationships.

Second, PS-1 has seen inclusion as central to the whole school and not about people with disabilities. Our mission statement says: "PS-1 will be a community of hospitality." Third, PS-1 is well connected to the everyday life of Denver. All kids, parents, and staff are constantly connected to all sorts of people, resources, and opportunities in the community. It is a community building school.

Annie has been a successful member of her school community. Annie will also always struggle with very real barriers. Her friend Peter is college bound, popular, dating, being phoned constantly by friends. Annie is telephoned occasionally by school friends, involved mostly through school activities rather than at other kids homes. Her next door neighbor friend Dana, who is five, no longer shares her interest in dolls and comes over less and less. She is usually just "a" friend rather than a best/close friend.

Annie cannot automatically "fit in". If left to herself she will lose her place in fast paced 1998 America. Annie needs to know that all of her is gifted - the part that loves to sing, the part that is best friends with Sara who is also called "mentally retarded", the part that looks forward to marriage and babies - all of Annie is a gift!

I used to be ashamed of Annie having many friends labeled as developmentally disabled. I wanted her in "normalized" settings and felt myself a failure when she was not in a "normalized" group. Now I find great peace by valuing diversity and meaning in her life. What Annie needs is what works. I also need the support of other parents and people who share Annie's vulnerability to exclusion. We need each other.

Annie has dreams of marriage, taking care of babies, and helping others. I believe she can realize these dreams by being a member of the community, rather than a 'client' of a human service system.

I am 51 years old. Annie's other parent figures are in their fifties. We will die. We will likely all die sooner than Annie. We are painfully aware that one day Annie will live without us. My great fear in life is that Annie will live her life as a 'client' rather than as a full community member. Most adults with developmental disabilities live in poverty, social isolation, clients with little self-determination. I want Annie to live with friends, adequate money, meaning, and real choices.

How will this happen? Families, friends and allies will seize the initiative and build strong communities. It is sad that human services have taken over community building for people with disabilities. It does not work. Human service's capacity is over-extended. The capacity of the larger community has barely been explored. Programs don't build community; people build community.

We are working in Denver to develop this kind of community building association. Members are using their connections, friends, and allies to mobilize the whole community to welcome people with disabilities into a future with safety, security, relationship, and meaning.

More money must be invested directly with families and communities rather than services and systems. Our family wants choice: resources, opportunities. We do not need supervision as clients. Annie's hope, and all our hopes for a good life are in the people of everyday life.

I describe our journey as both good and bad, joy and pain. I would choose no other life than ours. I am grateful for my daughter and our life together. I remember something Judith once said to me, "Every great gift has great suffering, and every great suffering has great gifts."

Tonight, I am aware of how grateful I am for this life with Annie. There is no one in life that I love or enjoy more. Acknowledging my fears, (rather than constant positive resolve), has given me peace and allowed me to open to my heart. I recognize her wonderful gifts. I see the inspiration Annie is to people like John McKnight. And, I also recognize her barriers, some which make her vulnerable.

I remember tonight a preacher's comments to me. He said, "You people talk about gifts and dreams rather than needs and deficiencies. This is good. But there is another part of life you guys do not talk much about. That is simply the part that "is". The plain old nature of living: birth, death, sickness, aging. Everything changes; nothing stays the same; the human condition."

And now I too recognize the importance of what just "is" in Annie's life.

Mike Green   (Annie's dad)

Read This Book...

This book is the wisdom of a woman who has been 44 years among us. It is a humbling book, because it makes me feel, at 62, as though I have been living in slow motion. How has she managed to do so much that she knows this much in only 44 years?

For anyone who has been near Judith, the answer is obvious for she burns so brightly. And this illumination lights her way through unexpected places.

In this book, you can follow the path she has explored. It is not a path cut through forests or forged across prairies. It is not a path won by feats over nature. Instead, it is a path created by nurture.

Judith's way is opened by dreaming. Along the way, gifted lives joint he journey. And when she finally arrives we see her dancing.

This book is Judith's invitation to join in the dance of life. She is graceful and lovely as she lights our lives and leads the way. You will never forget the joy and celebration of Judith's journey if you join her. And in the end, she will have led you out of disability into community.

John McKnight

John McKnight is a professor at North Western University in Chicago. He is a good friend of Judith and the Centre.

.Inclusion Press

24 Thorne Cres.
Toronto, Ont. M6H 2S5
Canada

INCLUSION PRESS INTERNATIONAL
ORDER FORM

24 Thome Crescent
Toronto, ON   Canada M6H 2S5
Tel 416-658-5363 Fax 416-658-5067
E-mail: 74640.1124@compuserve.com

WEB PAGE: http://inclusion.com

Oct. 1998 edition

Classic Videos

With a Little Help From My Friends
Prod: M. Forest & G. Flynn
The basics of creating schools where all kids belong and learn together. Hands on strategies – MAPS & Circles of Friends.

Kids Belong Together
Prod: People First Assoc of Lethbridge, Alta Featuring the late Fr. Patrick Mackan – a celebration of friendship – MAPS in action.

Together We're Better *Video*
Producer: Comforty Media Concepts
Staff Development Kit: a 2 hour video 3-pack of resources with Marsha Forest, Jack Pearpoint and Judith Snow demonstrating MAPS, PATH and CIRCLES. An inspiration.

Miller's MAP *Video*
Prod: Expectations Unltd &Inclusion Press
Children, parents, neighbors and professionals make inclusion happen– team facilitation and graphics in a MAP.

Friends of ...Clubs *Video*
Producers: Oregon Dept. of Education & University of Oregon A beautiful 15 min. story about creating community partnerships. Friends, friends, friends - the spark of life.

Dream Catchers *Video*
Producer: Institute on Disability, NH
New 16 minute video about dreams and circles of friends. Beautiful images, personal stories, images of the future. An inspiration.

Inclusion News
The Center publishes an independent annual newspaper - articles & resources you need . It has raving fans! International flair. Order in volume - $50 for a box of 150. A Conference Must!

Inclusion Exclusion Poster
by Jack Pearpoint
A vibrant eye catching 18" X 24" graphic poster exploring the why behind Inclusion and Exclusion.

New Videos! New Videos!

NEW WHEN SPIDER WEBS UNITE
☆ ★ ☆ **Shafik in Action**
Prod: Inclusion Press & Parashoot (35 min)
Shafik Asante - at the Toronto Summer Inst, July, 1996. Inspirational on community and inclusion. A tribute to a friend and colleague - includes the Shafik slide show.

Video

NEW PATH in ACTION
Team Building
☆ ★ **Training for Working with Groups**
Prod: Inclusion Press & Yellowknife Educ. Dist. 1 (65 minutes)
An inspiring & teaching video. Illustrates 2 Paths with 2 groups (40 high school students + senior administrators) planning the future of a school system. A must for anyone using PATH as a tool for Change.

Video

NEW PATH Training Video ☆
Introductory Path Training (with an individual)
Prod: Inclusion Press & Parashoot (35 min)
Exciting, creative, colorful futures planning tool. Jack & Marsha demonstrate 8 steps with Joe and his family. An excellent introduction - linked to the PATH book.

Video

NEW ☆ ☆ ALL MEANS ALL
the Inclusion Video
Prod: Video Journal & Inclusion Press
An outstanding introduction to Circles, MAPS and PATH. Produced by the Video Journal, this tape is a great beginning - showing all three major tools. (30 min)

Video

NEW ☆ Everyone Has a Gift
Building Communities of Capacity
Prod: Inclusion Press & Parashoot (60 min)
A JOHN McKNIGHT Keynote - the opening of the Toronto Summer Institute in July, 1996. McKnight at his finest.

Video

NEW New MAPS Training Video
☆ ☆ **SHAFIK'S MAP** ★ ☆
Prod: Inclusion Press & Parashoot
MAPS- step by step - John O'Brien facilitating Shafik Asante's Map. How to make families partners in planning. Holistic, creative, colorful futures planning for people, families, organizations. + Judith Snow on Dreaming. (45 min)

Video

Friendship: It's About Time
Video
Produced by Vision TV, Exec. Prod: Rita Deverell, Prod: Sadia Zaman
★ 27 minute video exploration of friendship: joys, heartaches & maintenance, featuring Marsha, Jack and Judith. ★

Courses for your consideration...

Come to the 4th Annual
TORONTO Summer Institute
Inclusion, Community & Diversity
July 3-9, 1999

Hosts for the Learning Community:
- John McKnight
- John O'Brien
- Marsha Forest
- Jack Pearpoint
- Wayne Helgason
- Judith Snow
- Bahiya Cabral Asante
- Nkosi Asante
- Dave Hinsberger(1 day)

The Creative Facilitator

A four day hands-on course
to learn and practice
Circles, MAPS, PATH,
Solution Circles,
Graphic Recording
and Process Facilitation
Jan. 27-30, 1999

Available in Toronto or on the Road

And don't forget,
Inclusion News

Design for Change

A Course that moves you "out
of the box" and "commissions"
each participant to design their
future the way they really want
it to be. A powerful exploration
of the future of change. 25
participants - Maximum!!
Feb. 23-26, 1999

Warning: These courses may
change your life.

For Information Contact:
Cathy Hollands, General Manager
or Marsha Forest and Jack Pearpoint
INCLUSION PRESS International
24 Thorne Crescent
Toronto, Ontario   M6H 2S5
Tel: 416-658-5363 Fax: 416-658-5067
E-mail: 74640.1124@compuserve.com
Web Page: http://www.inclusion.com

Visit our WEB
PAGE:
http://
inclusion.com

All Means All!

Don't Defend Inclusion:
Make Others Defend
Segregation!

The Centre gratefully acknowledges the generous support of the
Imperial Oil Charitable Foundation
for supporting our commitment to inclusion.

Imperial Oil